W9-AAT-431

Praise for
CHANGING THE CONVERSATION

Changing the Conversation is an "absolute must-read" book for individuals, families and business owners who want to preserve, protect and empower their "true wealth" as a legacy for generations. Through Gary Klaben's powerful process, you will experience a meaningful transformation—greater clarity, balance, focus and confidence in your life. His leadership and masterful communication provide new direction and capability. Get ready to gain tremendous insights that will transform your life and true wealth for generations.

~Douglas R. Andrew
Best-Selling Author of the Missed Fortune *book series*
Paramount Financial Services, Inc.

Through real-life examples and being a visionary practitioner of his craft, Gary has created a process that is both revolutionary and fundamental for financial advisory practices. *Changing the Conversation* offers a masterful new tool to advisors eager and alert to ways to help clients move forward.

~James Barnash, CFP®
President, James A. Barnash & Associates

Changing the Conversation provides the common man with the tools to successfully attack the future. Klaben, a cross between Dave Ramsey and Peter Drucker, provides a thought-provoking self-examination of how we can change our life journey for the better. This book will make a difference.

~Edmund Dowling
Vice President, Quantum Research International, Inc.

In his endearing, optimistic tone, Klaben showcases the desire we all have for our families' future, by engaging in a long-overdue conversation about steps to personal and financial health in the 21st century.

~*Curtis Estes*
Author of Your Life By Design
(A Step-by-Step Guide to Creating a Bigger Future)
Insurance Agent, Northwestern Mutual

Gary makes a strong case that we often overstate the importance of our financial inheritance at the expense of the more satisfying emotional and intellectual inheritance we can pass on to our offspring—which sustains financial health over time. *Changing the Conversation* helped me refocus my goals to include all of the above....This book reads like a wonderful book on tape. I almost literally can hear Gary's insights being spoken.

~*Dave Goss, CPA*
President, EPAS, LLC

Gary Klaben has authored a book that is both visionary and practical. He sets out a practical strategy to correct multifaceted individual, family and social issues in a clear, concise manner. *Changing the Conversation* ought to be made required reading for Americans from high school age upwards. Gary Klaben is an exceptional leader, author and American. America needs to carefully listen to this man...and learn.

~*Charles Lynn Lowder, Chief Executive Officer*
Chief Compliance Officer, Everest, LLC

Changing the Conversation is a step-by-step guide for bridging to a financially and personally rewarding future for both individuals and families.

~*Philip Tirone*
Author of 7 Steps to a 720 Credit Score
President, 720CreditScore.com
The Mortgage Equity Group

With half of my clients being family businesses, I see many wealth-related issues. This book is a masterpiece in helping you understand managing, transferring and protecting family wealth.

~*Gino Wickman*
Author of Traction: Get A Grip On Your Business
Creator of EOS®, President, EOS Worldwide

In *Changing the Conversation,* the reader will experience first-hand how much Gary Klaben cares about his clients personally and how he challenges his clients to envision the best versions of themselves today and in the future. This book is a great read; enjoy and grow.

~*Joseph Zarlengo, Attorney*
Asset Protection and Estate Tax Planning
Chicago, Illinois

CHANGING THE CONVERSATION

CHANGING THE CONVERSATION

Transformational Steps to
Financial and Family Well-Being

Gary Klaben

Let's keep up the conversation!

Gary Klaben

CHANGING THE CONVERSATION

Copyright © 2010 by Gary Klaben

Library of Congress Control Number: 2010909120

ISBN: Hardcover 978-0-9828009-0-4

Cover design: Gwyn Kennedy Snider

Book design: Jessica Poisl

Text font: Adobe Jenson™ Pro

Chapter headlines: Adobe Penumbra™ Sans

Initial caps: Engravers™, The Monotype Corporation

Engraving: *Castanea dentata*, American chestnut. *Plants*, Dover Publications, Inc., Mineola, NY, 1988

Printing: Malloy Incorporated

This book was printed in the United States of America.

For more information, contact:

Navigator Press, Inc.

847.730.1760

orders@navigatorpressinc.com

2700 Patriot Blvd. - Suite 440

Glenview, IL 60026

www.changingtheconversationthebook.com

To Debra – thanks for listening.

"*Always do right. This will gratify some people, and astonish the rest.*"

– Mark Twain

Table of Contents

Introduction 1

Personal Journey 10

Changing the Conversation—Part 1 22

Financial Awareness 34

Do You Have the Right KASH? 48

The Moment Is Now....................................60

How the Brain Learns 69

Getting Started to Getting Started 81

Do the Correct Thing 90

The Psychology of Money............................102

Mine the Minds of Mentors 111

Are You a Chief or Indian?........................ 121

Are You Lucky?.. 130

Buying into America 143

Understanding Complexity—And Taming It 153

Navigating Storms and Currents 163

Age of Art and Heart 172

Retirement Yearning 184

What Is Your True Worth? 196

Whose Property Do You Own? 209

We're Better Together 221

Pass It On 229

What 'To Live' Really Means 240

Growing Greatness 251

Money, Money, Money 264

Changing the Conversation—Part 2 276

Bibliography 284

Acknowledgments 289

Introduction

Individuals need more than mere things.

They need trusted guidance.

There has never been a more urgent time to discuss the perplexing issues surrounding family and financial well-being.

In 2010, we as a nation are struggling with a slowly recovering economy and a crisis in confidence. The last quarter of 2008 was a severe shock to our economic system, forcing us to question the financial strength of the United States. For all of our financial power, democratic freedoms and sense of unlimited possibilities, we today gaze upon devastated companies, broken families and disconnected communities. We feel isolated, confused and powerless. We have lost our certainty and nerve.

Strong leadership is vital to winning back our confidence.

It is very important to have leadership in government, industry, media, community and family. We need genuine people in authority who serve us and engender our trust, allowing us to grow affirmatively in our chosen work or avocation.

Over the past 40 years, there has been a slow degradation of genuine natural authority within the United States. For those born after World War II, the war cry in the late '60s was not to trust anyone over age 30. The cultural revolution that ensued rejected "authority," and especially the government leadership at the time, the Johnson and Nixon administrations. Police officers were called "pigs," military personnel were spat on, and flags and draft cards were burned. It wasn't that most young people rejected authority per se, but the perceived authoritarianism they saw all around them.

There is a very distinct difference between authority and authoritarianism. The root of *authority* is *augment* and *author*, and the Latin *augere* means "to create, to enlarge, to make able to grow." Authoritarianism is the opposite of growth, which is enabled by authority. By defending the status quo, authoritarianism hinders and restricts human growth and freedom.

It is parents, teachers and mentors who "author" the growth of their charges through their positions of authority. In the '60s, America's youth perceived an impervious and invidious authoritarianism being forced upon them by all who represented the establishment. Television shows such as "Father Knows Best" and "The Andy Griffith Show" were rejected for a lifestyle of drugs, sex, and rock and roll. As was the case in the Revolutionary War, the Civil War, and the union and suffragette movements, the cultural revolution was simply another movement in a long history of Americans reinventing themselves.

Americans own the role of rugged individualism in the world. We seek out new ideas without the restraints seen in other authoritarian cultures that can snatch away freedoms at any moment for any reason. By the early 1980s, the erstwhile hippies and draft dodgers were wearing business suits and holding down positions of authority they had rejected earlier.

Today we are experiencing revolution of a different type. It started slowly when the tech bubble burst in 2000. This time, the American institutions under attack are government, industry and media. These major

U.S. institutions have sorely disappointed us. Rampant government malfeasance runs the gamut from prostitution scandal to corruption: New York Gov. Spitzer and Illinois Gov. Blagojevich, to name but a few—one resigned and the other impeached for his alleged illegal activities. As citizens, we have come to not trust or respect our politicians, and some even regard them as a democracy's necessary evil.

In 2001, we discovered that Bernie Ebbers of WorldCom and Kenneth Lay of Enron had built large publicly traded companies that were essentially a sham. The fall of these two giants devastated the retirement plans for hundreds of thousands of employees. As for much of the U.S. media, this has, unfortunately, now become mainstream entertainment. The marketing and promotional focus is oft-times to drive a wedge between the American people, polarizing a stark choice either to the left or the right. No longer is there a reasonable middle and discerning discussion. You are either with me or against me.

What we now have is a capitalism revolution.

We are desperately looking for leadership in the form of natural authority. This needs to be restored at all levels of our American institutions. The trust and authority we once knew needs to be regained. We need politicians who are true servants of the people and who enact legislation that meets people's needs—not line private pockets or curry favor with political pork. We need corporate leaders who cut their pay in bad times to keep workers employed rather than host lavish parties while Rome burns. We need courageous news media who once again practice investigative, hard-news journalism without the empty, bombastic cant and agenda-driven spin.

We want to trust our leaders again. They can only gain our trust through dedicated service, consistent hard work, and by acting responsibly for the good of the people they lead.

The deep 2008-09 recession and resulting economic turmoil in the financial markets and banks resulted from our government being asleep at the regulatory wheel, from shady mortgage brokers, and from greedy Wall Street money firms—all three combining to create a huge abuse of debt. This dereliction of fiscal duty has undermined our confidence in the pillars of capitalism.

Capitalism, in actuality, has never really been about capital. Rather, capitalism's bedrock involves the trust and cooperation of a free democratic people at a much higher level of group participation. We know there are plenty of people who know how to run the numbers. What we don't know is how many people understand the level of emotional intelligence and ethical cooperation necessary to build a better nation, not squander what we have already gained.

The microchip has drastically changed our world, and not necessarily for the better. Thirty years ago, we had a better sense of community. A civic-minded young man or woman joined a community organization such as Rotary International, the Lions Club or the local Chamber of Commerce. They met weekly, gained a sense of community, and began to take ownership of local issues and projects. They were mentored by those with gray hair who had sustained the bumps and bruises of life experiences. Simply put, back then, people interacted and socialized more often with associates and friends in many different ways.

In Robert Putnam's insightful book, *Bowling Alone: The Collapse and Revival of American Community* (2000), he studied these social changes and their effect on our society. One of many examples: Although the number of people who bowl has increased over the 20-year period he studied, the number of bowling leagues has decreased. If people bowl alone, they do not interact with others. They certainly are not discussing civic issues, which affect the larger community. Today's young people socialize on Facebook, MySpace, Twitter and LinkedIn—if they have time left over after answering their BlackBerrys and e-mails, or after text messaging and blogging. One's real community is waning, and social trust continues to fade.

What do trust and authority have to do with money? Plenty. Currency, money and the essence of money are part of our American way of life. They may be seen as pure capitalism, but encompass far more than that. Many countries around the world are built on capitalism, but they are not the same as the United States. The key element in the "wealth" of a nation is its culture combined with capitalism. Presently we are undergoing a capitalism revolution. As I write this, wealth is being redefined.

American culture is more dynamically rooted in change, more diverse, and more likely to alter direction more often than any other country. The hallmark of U.S. capitalism is seeking competitive advantage and continual retooling, innovation and progress.

For example, the world has watched our society change, morph and reinvent itself through our foreign policy. In *Special Providence: American Foreign Policy and How It Changed the World* (2001), Walter Russell Mead describes the four guiding philosophies that have influenced the formation of American foreign policy. From Hamilton's focus on commerce, to Jefferson's eye on our founding principles, to Jackson's preoccupation with military power, to Wilson's ideal of a just world order, America's leaders have "shifted" among these four foreign policy gears—sometimes double-shifting and riding the clutch, but other times solidly adhering to one philosophical gear.

To many Europeans watching this, Americans appear to be haphazard, fickle, inconsistent, headstrong, fiercely independent, obsessed with commerce and money, and most certainly "uncultured." Yet—this is a good thing! We constantly try out new things, experiment and probe, readily reject what doesn't work, and build up what does work.

We are embarking on that journey of transition right now.

This book will look at how wealth and money find their way into our lives, both literally and viscerally. We move through life cycles of learning when we are young, earning in our middle years, and yearning later in life. At each stage, there is a different focus, a different education, and a different role that we play—particularly for those we touch such as family.

Learning, earning and *yearning* is a life journey of discovery. How we elect to experience each phase—in relation to money—will determine if money's immense power, in turn, empowers us or makes us its master.

Money, after all, stands at the crossroads of all human existence, material and social progress, economic growth, political power, a citizen's empathy and a society's greatness. America's journey continues to change—money's role continues to change with it. Just as who and what we are as Americans evolves over time—always a bit elusive and difficult to pin down—so, too, does money pose its own unique and evolving challenges.

This book's intent: Through each cycle of your life, to help you wisely anticipate life's inevitable changes and, by understanding the changing role of money over time, find both financial growth and personal satisfaction.

Personal Journey

If I've learned any single thing over the past near half century, it is that when it comes to money, most of us have some sort of hang-up about it.

We sometimes get overwhelmed dealing with a seemingly endless number of money issues.

As we move through life, things change for us—emotionally, psychologically and spiritually. That applies to dealing with money issues, too. We constantly try to integrate money suitably into life's equation, whether it be our daily interactions with family, friends or co-workers. More time passes and we continue to grow, refine our thinking, and revise our priorities. As we change, so does our relationship with money.

Like you, my personal awareness of money began when very young. Like you, my life's journey of involvement with money has undergone profound changes.

As a child of the 1960s, I received an allowance of a dime weekly from my mother. She and my dad wanted us to learn the value of money. This was a good starting place.

Shortly after receiving one of my weekly allowances, Mom asked me what I had done with it. I told her I gave the dime to Mark, a neighbor pal of mine.

Well, Mom was furious. She demanded to know why I would give money away instead of saving it for the right occasion. I tried to explain that Mark was my buddy, that he'd craved a candy bar but had no money, and that I'd given him my dime.

My mom's focus on that particular day was not on neighborly charity and good works. She sternly informed me I was losing my allowance for a month. Money doesn't grow on trees. Her son needed a swift, rude reminder of his imprudent money decision.

Did I learn my mother's money lesson? Yes—and no. Like you, I continue to give to others as the need and occasion arises. That should make any mother proud— at least if candy bars aren't involved. But as for my pal Mark's sudden craving for milk chocolate, caramel and nuts, Mom's lesson about the possible misuse of money has never been lost on me.

Growing up as I did in a crowded household with nine siblings—that's right, our folks had 10 children—the matter of money commanded attention. When I turned 11, I was able to start my own paper route. I enjoyed the deliveries and saying hi to all my customers. I made $20 a week in tips and learned how to serve my customers well. It was an early life lesson about how to determine and meet the needs of others in a commercial venture. Later, when I turned 16, I began working in a local bakery full-time in the summer, while also continuing my paper route with the help of my siblings.

My mom—with 10 high-spirited youngsters tripping over each other in a three-bedroom home that included only two baths—imposed Spartan training camp rules. She had to—her very sanity was on the line!

As a family, we GI'd the entire home once a week. House rule: No posters on walls. With my four brothers, I shared one clothes closet, one dresser (chest of drawers) and one box of toys. Beds were made, rugs lint-picked (by hand), and bathrooms cleaned before setting off for school each morning.

Mom kept us very busy. In high school, I ran cross-country, indoor track and outdoor track; worked my paper route; and cleaned the house on weekends. At home and in the community, we learned a strong work ethic, independence, confidence, and how to organize our busy schedules.

Still, as I approached my senior year in high school, I knew quite well there was very little money available for the next stage of life, college.

That particular money issue sent me looking for college scholarships and other possible "full-ride" opportunities. Fortunately for me, I earlier had visited the United States Military Academy at West Point, New York, during my sophomore year. My cross-country coach's son was a cadet there and we had visited him.

What an incredible place! I came away with a burning desire to be there: the spectacular parade ground situated high above the majestic Hudson River, everything "The Point" stood for—duty, honor, country. I wanted that!

Moreover, my mother's no-nonsense, 18-year "boot camp" prepared me admirably. If I were fortunate enough to be accepted, the money problem would be solved. A West Point education is paid for by the government.

And—I was accepted. Over the next four years, West Point educated me, re-emphasized the lessons of hard work and persistence, conditioned me both physically and mentally, and polished my character by instilling a military code of ethics and integrity.

Upon graduation from West Point, I entered the United States Army as a brand-new Second Lieutenant Infantry Officer.

Alaska was my first assignment. My Fairbanks duty station in winter was a far cry from the popular tourist image of kayaking and humpback whale watching in glacial bays. Upon arrival, I immediately confronted a "money issue" with my enlisted troops. The 18-to-21-year-old soldiers seemed particularly prone to money problems. One soldier, upon arriving in Alaska, went out his first weekend and wrote checks for furniture, stereo equipment and many other items until, literally, he ran out of checks. Incredibly, the soldier—fresh out of basic training—thought that so long as he had checks, he had money in his checking account!

Mentoring him—and other soldiers and non-commissioned officers—I periodically sat down and helped them plan how to save money for a new car, structure the purchase of their first house, and make sure their powers of attorney were set up to allow their spouses access to accounts if they were immediately sent into combat.

One soldier's question revealed a spark of Yankee ingenuity—he asked me what it took to buy a business. Just before he resigned from the U.S. Army to take a union job with Alyeska—the company that operates the Alaska Pipeline—we sat down to review his offer. We determined he could save $100,000 in three years, return to the "lower 48," and purchase his business.

I greatly enjoyed my five years in the Army. Still, I was impatient to try my own hand in the business world. My first job? Project leader for computer programmers in the management information system (MIS) department of a large public company. A few months after entering civilian life, I obtained my real estate license, to better understand the field and to begin bidding on FHA and VA foreclosures. All of these activities expanded my breadth of knowledge about money.

But—something was missing. My business job wasn't very fulfilling. In addition, I came to realize that I needed to learn much, much more about how to make money and run a successful business.

Fortunately, during this time of my life, I had not yet hung up my "green suit" entirely, so I drilled regularly with a military reserve unit at Fort Sheridan, Illinois, north of Chicago.

One day, my military boss surprised me with a question: "Gary, how happy are you with your civilian profession?" I replied, "Oh, it's all right—not exactly what I expected."

He suggested I meet with a financial-planner friend of his. "A financial planner?" I responded. "What's that?" He sought to explain, and then introduced me to his buddy. As his friend outlined financial planning to me, suddenly a light clicked on. "Financial planning—that's been the common denominator of all my life experiences."

Almost immediately, it hit me: Running a business that involves planning (which I enjoy), learning about money (which requires continual education), and working with families (which carries all the way back to my boyhood paper-route days) defines my dream job.

I started as an insurance agent specializing in financial planning. The year was 1986. From the very start, I was enthralled with the whole universe of money issues—from income taxes to investments to planning for estates, retirement and philanthropy.

Money is omnipresent in our lives—it's compulsory and inescapable. If "death and taxes" are givens, then money is the interstitial glue that binds our obligations and dreams together and keeps us whole during good times and bad.

My thirst for new insights has always been insatiable. Early on, I jumped in with both feet to learn as much about money as possible. Over the first decade, I completed one course after another. Even as Debra and I began experiencing the joys of new parenthood (including the messy diapers and nighttime colic), I set aside weekends and worked diligently at reading financial textbooks. Eventually, I received certificates as a Chartered Financial Consultant (ChFC) and Chartered Life Underwriter (CLU), and a master's degree in Financial Services (MSFS).

That decade remains vivid in my memory—watching our daughter Sarah and son John take their first tentative steps and soon hop on their school bus—and, of course, meeting daily with many different families about their money matters.

So many challenging issues to discuss and solve. —The

airline pilot who died on his retirement date. —The woman swindled out of her $4 million inheritance by her brother. Each family situation proved unique.

Thankfully, there were many happy, lighter moments, too. Some client parents wanted their young children to learn good money habits early. We met and discussed ways to teach financial discipline. Today many of these children are adults, married, with their own homes and successful careers.

For every family who has been mentored and coached about money and financial planning, there proportionately are scores of other families who seemingly "never get around to it."

Family stories about success and failure with money are legendary.

Families whom I have counseled over the years, the clients I have served, comprise a vast reservoir of learned financial knowledge and pragmatic money experience. If life is a laboratory, then all that I have mastered has gone directly into ways to help my clients grow.

My personal journey from learning to understanding to meaning to substance did not happen overnight. Far from it!

Changing the Conversation

Besides being a laboratory, life is also a journey. All of us are time travelers through life's ups and downs. Even now, after decades of financial-planner experience, I continue to learn, test, anticipate change and quickly respond to it.

Eternal vigilance. There can be no alternative.

The real "meaning of money" never even dawned on me until I came to realize that one must look beyond the visible.

Take the example of your house. Walk around it—what do you see? Floors, walls, ceilings, doorways, of course—and by your personal choices of furniture, artwork, family photos, paint, wallpaper, light fixtures, window coverings and accessories, you have made the house your home.

If you're like me, you probably haven't given much thought to your home's invisible infrastructure: the studded walls, roof and floor joists, reinforced concrete foundation and weather-resistant exterior that ensure personal safety from all seasons of weather. This is the real strength of the house, without which the whole structure would tumble down with the first storm.

Money is the same way. We look at our securities portfolios, 401(k)s, tax returns, checking and savings accounts without peering more deeply into what is really going on behind the scene.

Financial commentator, writer, actor and TV personality Ben Stein, when interviewed on "CBS Sunday Morning," joked that there are only two things one ever needs to know about money: the printed currency's numerals and their velocity of disappearance. Sure, with a bit of humor, he was just making an obvious point about the cash we have, and the rate we choose to spend it to maintain our lifestyle.

Beyond the visible, day-to-day flow of money through our busy lives lurks the invisible drivers that decide money's meaning for us, and that determine our money fate.

What you and I fall short on, all too often, is dealing with money emotionally, psychologically, even spiritually.

Remember former Philippines First Lady Imelda Marcos and her gazillion pairs of shoes? —Pure addiction! Ponzi schemer Bernie Madoff and his $65 billion-plus hoax? —Pursuing stature, power and greed! Heavyweight boxer Michael Tyson ending up penniless after so many multi-million-dollar prize fights? —Completely out of control!

You see, it's all about the money...and...it's not about

the money.

Managing the interrelationships of needs, wants, happiness, giving, gratitude and self-esteem, as these issues relate to money, poses a continual challenge. Researching, testing and implementing successful techniques and habits that strengthen one's ability to handle money in the context of one's life—that is a life quest.

This book is a journey from dependency to mastery. It is a journey of self-discovery as well as a how-to guide to financial self-realization. It is the many conversations about what really matters and how to think, prioritize and act.

Don't worry if at first you can't perceive the road ahead. The choices and options of putting money "to work" will reveal themselves soon enough, as the many illusory benefits hiding beneath the fabric of money are revealed and evaluated.

Over time, as you become more familiar with how to interact with today's complex financial world, you will gain shrewd mastery over the key elements of money: its *substance* as well as *essence*.

It's time to get started.

Changing the Conversation—Part 1

Over the years, we have had many conversations with our clients.

These conversations have been evermore varied following the global financial debacle in 2008-2009.

Our large financial bureaucracies are full of very smart people, but separately lack the cohesiveness to deliver integrated products and services. Frankly, they are quite out of control.

The long-standing titans of American financial power appear arrogant, greedy, slow to change, and out of touch with society.

There is a call to change—to *change the conversation*. Fundamentally alter the way we communicate with one another.

Changing the Conversation

The Internet has made very visible a financial emperor with no clothes: the practice of large financial institutions to be product-centered versus client-centered, commission versus fee, sales versus consultative.

We no longer accept being the pawn in the complex financial chess match, with little consideration given to our needs, wants and desires.

Scientists tell us that the Earth's magnetic poles reverse every 30,000 to 300,000 years. By analogy, we're seeing the delivery of today's financial services switch from a "push" to a "pull."

For thousands of years, products were sold or pushed on to consumers. The companies that manufactured those products, from stocks to shoelaces, did so with the belief that consumers would readily buy them. It used to be so much simpler when the cobbler knew the nuances of your feet and the tailor the unique dimensions of your body.

Today, everything is manufactured based on surveys, focus groups, trend analyses, and what products may sell better than a competitor's. There is a disconnect, or distancing, from the end consumer.

{ 23 }

This may be okay for purchasing a pair of shoes or slacks—but as for our money? We no longer want to be pushed to purchase.

We want a relationship. —A relationship that begins with a conversation well-grounded in authority and trust. —A conversation that is about *us*. —A conversation that leads to a tailored solution based on our specific needs. That adds value. That fulfills a purpose. We want to be convincingly yet gently pulled to a decision.

We need another kind of conversation today.

Ask yourself: Why do most companies and organizations fail to embrace user-centered approaches?

Are the inherent defects of today's transactions marking the imminent demise of managerial capitalism as we know it?

In its place, can a new business logic emerge that links an economy based on personal relationships and the ubiquitous Internet to provide a better advocacy and deep support for individuals?

Aren't wise advocacy and deep support the things that are missing in our 21st century, speeded-up, fragmented, computerized, gadgetized world?

Please know—*you* are not the problem.

The barriers to workability are rooted in today's antiquated models of business life that fail to align business interests with the interests of individuals and families.

As authors Shoshana Zuboff and James Maxmin explain in *The Support Economy: Why Corporations Are Failing Individuals and the Next Episode of Capitalism* (2002), no corporate executive or strategy consultant can spark a customer-centered revolution as long as they operate from within an organization that is based on current business structures and goals. This disturbing assertion is not made carelessly, but is based on findings of Zuboff's exhaustive research, sponsored by Harvard Business School.

The book opens with this declaration: "People have changed more than the business organizations upon which they depend. The last fifty years have seen the rise of a new breed of individuals, yet corporations continue to operate according to a logic invented at the time of their origin, a century ago. The chasm that now separates individuals and organizations is marked by frustration, mistrust, disappointment, and even rage. It also harbors the possibility of a new capitalism and a new era of wealth creation" (p. 3).

Elaborating on this opening, Zuboff and Maxmin describe the individual as "history's shock absorber," caught between opposing historical forces. While individuals search for psychological self-determination, organizations sap time and freedom from employees and withhold service and support from consumers, all in the endless pursuit for cost-efficient (i.e., value-starved) transactions.

Zuboff and Maxmin argue that this "transaction starvation" leads to loss of care.

"(This) explains the callous shrugs we receive from airline employees during our frantic attempts to negotiate with airline bureaucracies when our flights are cancelled," writes book reviewer Peter Morville about *The Support Economy* for SIGCHI Bulletin. "Airline employees are not bad people. They have simply entered a state of learned helplessness. This also explains our frustrations with the healthcare industry, corporate Web sites and customer service in general, and suggests that our rising appetite for large houses, home schooling and self-employment are actually indicators of people seeking refuge from a growing societal malaise."

Anyone desiring to restore the "user experience" should read this book, if only for the critical analysis of present obstacles to customer-centered approaches. Zuboff and Maxmin cast the frenzied zeal surrounding the Internet in the 1990s as a symptom of "pent-up demand for sanctuary, voice, and connection" (p. 289). Yet they add that a pervasive digital world is an insufficient ingredient in the recipe for a new economy.

Transformation from the self-support model of today's Web to the deep support model of tomorrow's "federated networks" requires a new logic—a new conversation.

Zuboff and Maxmin propose a set of principles that describe this new enterprise logic, and that place individuals at the center and organizations at the periphery of wealth-creation processes.

This is a Copernican revolution for the economy that is "the commercial equivalent of the Vietnam Veterans Memorial Wall...[which] reflects the great psychological reformation of the second half of the twentieth century" (p. 324).

The Support Economy offers various examples and

scenarios, but falls short of painting a picture of this new economy and the path that will lead us there. But that's okay. The authors are defining a road yet largely untraveled. The book is intended as a wake-up call, alerting us to better options still hidden in uncharted territory.

To emphasize: We must change the conversation. The push of financial products is old school, faded, pre-Internet. The pull of meaning, values and purposes is post-financial crisis, back-to-basics and client-centered.

The consumer is now in the driver's seat.

Many of us are unaware that this fundamental role reversal has occurred. Consider during Medieval times the knight in his shining armor on his powerful steed. He was a formidable foe. Then along came technological change, the invention of gunpowder. —More precisely, the application of gunpowder to a musket. This one change defeated the knight's armor and forever relegated it to technological obsolescence.

In a recent film comedy, "He's Just Not That Into You," Drew Barrymore plays Mary, a single lady looking for Mr. Right. During one scene, Mary expresses frustration about a possible new relationship, saying: "I had this guy leave me a voicemail at work, so I called him at home, and then he e-mailed me to my BlackBerry, and so I texted his cell, and now I have to go around checking all these different portals just to get rejected by seven different technologies. It's exhausting!"

Mary, like many of us, is terribly exasperated dealing with the whole "being single" thing. Well, back when I was dating, we either left a phone message or wrote a letter. Pretty simple. The bad news today is: Our lives have become more complex, we are more frustrated, and we feel powerless to make a change.

All this was brought about by the tiny, seemingly insignificant microchip. It's the saga of gunpowder all over again. During the Middle Ages, the strategies and tactics of warfare were forced to change. The microchip is forcing us to change as well.

What's needed is support—*deep support*. That can only happen if we get to know one another. If we build relationships. —If we delve meaningfully into the complex, frustrating parts of our financial, multigenerational lives. A conversation must happen and it must be about people—you and your family.

In today's world, we must change the conversation.

Fortuitously, the microchip has brought us technologies that can help make the complex simple, that can turn frustrations into opportunities, and that can help us take control of our lives.

Deep support is needed now more than ever due to the backdrop of increased uncertainty. We're uncertain about our state and federal governments, about terrorism striking at the heart of America, about our children's and grandchildren's futures, and another market bubble or major loss for our investments.

With deep support and clear conversation, one can attain preparedness, proper perspective, and reliable clarity amidst a chaotic world. It is the continual conversation, grounded in knowledge and trust, that bestows confidence. Solid, authoritative advice from knowing the client well provides vision and direction.

There used to be a time in this country when the carriage trade received deep support from bank trust departments. Over many generations, a cache of dedicated bankers and trust officers saw to every detail and played a vital service role. They serviced a select few wealthy

Americans. Those dedicated long-term bankers and seasoned trust departments are long gone. They were gobbled up by one too many bank mergers that squeezed the deep support out of the system for greater profits and "shareholder value."

Based on the recent financial scandals, there clearly needs to be a return to financial sanity, accountability and utmost integrity.

The role of the long-term financial advisor with multigenerational family ties must be re-established. It is already happening with the emergence of multi-family offices, life planners and comprehensive financial advisors.

When a relationship is established, it should be for multiple generations. This surely will help thwart the needless financial-wealth destruction cycle of "shirtsleeves to shirtsleeves" in three generations. Time and time again, would-be financial advisors have watched helplessly as the wealth builders passed assets to the wealth freezers and finally to the wealth spenders. —A terrible downward spiral toward human misery and suffering, needlessly brought about by the abuse of money.

Each of the chapters that follow are "conversations." Each

will address a different timely topic. Each will focus on how "the conversation is changing"—and how to anticipate change, prepare to manage it, and even lead it.

In the pages ahead, we will explore financial and family planning, relationships, mentoring, trained habits, meaning and values, purpose and legacy, and much more.

This book offers transformational steps to financial and family well-being—a new platform for understanding what actually drives the practical deployment of money.

We will pursue the more arcane subjects of complexity and philanthropy. We will explore the ups and downs of retirement, and the ins and outs of communication. We will look at what will replace the dashing knight in shining armor and the venerable old-line bank trust officer.

It's critical we begin to *change the conversation*. Today, frankly, many aspects of modern life are broken and can't be fixed. Many business and organizational interactions have grown hopelessly out of touch with the people they should be serving. A new society of individuals no longer accepts the traditional rules of engagement.

Instead of tired, antiquated ideas, people hunger for new relationships of trusted expert advocacy that afford deep support for their complex lives.

The chapters of conversations that follow seek to provide a profound new structure for framing and addressing the future. Drawing upon the many varied professional experiences working with our clients over the past three decades, we will probe their individual stories for fresh insights. These insights, in turn, can lead to highly innovative applications.

Conversations need to change. This book is a call to action for individuals, for families, for clients, for financial advisors—indeed, for every citizen who cares about the long-term future.

Financial Awareness

$\mathbf{A}$bout 15 years ago, I was completing a plan to help a client consolidate and organize all of the financial affairs for him and his wife. They were in their late 60s and had two children in their mid-40s and several grandchildren. I was driving home after they had signed all of their legal documents in line with this new plan, which would save their estate about $2 million in death taxes.

Suddenly I began to have a bad sinking feeling. I couldn't quite put my finger on it. Was there something concerning me at home about my wife, my children, my friends and extended family? No. Was there something I forgot to do? No. Then what was it?

Just then it hit me. My client was reducing their death taxes, which meant the couple's children would be receiving an additional $1 million each. But these children were not ready to handle an additional $1 million, let alone the remainder of this nice estate. They simply were ill-equipped to deal with this amount of money. Were they spendthrifts? No. I had met them. They were living within their means. But they had very few accumulated assets. Would they act wisely with sudden wealth?

I wanted to turn my car around immediately, return to my office, and destroy the documents. I did not want to be a party to this "crime"—a crime of money abuse perpetrated on one's children because of their lack of understanding about money and money matters. I envisioned them possibly turning out like many entertainers and athletes who are in the public eye, with broken personal lives brought about by fame and money.

This was my "Eureka!" moment. I realized there needed to be multigenerational education and assimilation of both the good and bad about money and money issues.

Is money the root of all evil? Money is the second-most discussed topic in the Bible. Are a fool and his money soon parted? Certainly, those who are inexperienced with money may make some very bad choices. Is it a sin to be poor? Abuse, including money abuse that results in a poor state of mind, is unhealthy. Is a penny saved a penny earned? Yes—but should you put all your eggs in one basket?

We've all heard these common sayings, along with many others repeated daily throughout our lives. Uncle Al said to never invest in the stock market. Look at what happened to all those dopes who got caught in the 1929-1933 stock market crash! Aunt Sally said never buy real estate after the family experienced the farmers' Dust Bowl disaster of the 1930s.

Should you buy only used cars? Is the bank the only secure place to invest? Are stocks and bonds truly safe investments? Should you be concerned about inflation or deflation? Should you always pay cash for everything? How much should you set aside for a rainy day? Should you always ask multiple questions and consider multiple answers on every pending money situation?

Let's face it—we all are a little weird about money. For most of us, this weirdness is based on our experience and our level of understanding about money.

The secret to incorporating money wisely into our lives is to start teaching our youth as soon as possible. If you are reading this as a young adult, the secret is not to wait, but to start learning about financial matters now. All learning begins when we decide to grow. For some, it may be about money basics, and for others, more experience about mentoring or teaching our youth.

Politics and religion are the supposed taboo subjects at cocktail parties. In most American households, the topic of secrecy is money. When I was growing up, we didn't really talk about money, other than to lament that we didn't have much of it.

Coming from a large family, my parents practiced just-in-time financing. That is, Dad's paycheck every two weeks was virtually gone the day after payday, and somehow Mom made things work for another two weeks. We had no debt, other than the $11,000 mortgage on our home purchased in the early 1950s. Life was much simpler, with one-tenth the distractions that bombard our youth in today's high-information society.

Remember when our moms kicked us out of the house and told us not to come back until dinnertime? Do you recall sitting down for a long family conversation or a game of checkers, or just spending a rainy day inside reading a good book?

Today it's just too easy to get your hands on money, even

though you might not have sufficient household income to pay it back.

Years ago when my parents needed to expand our small, two-bedroom, Cape Cod house (our family had grown from six to seven children), a visit to our hometown banker was required. This banker, who approved our mortgage 10 years earlier, proceeded to remind my parents of all the evils of debt. He forewarned that an additional $5,000 for a home remodeling could be the undoing of our life. This additional debt burden might actually cause us to end up on the street.

Today, of course, many people feel entitled to their rehab houses with all the modern amenities, regardless of whether they have budgeted accordingly. Somehow, inexplicably, they delude themselves into thinking that they can just squeeze by unnoticed. When people cover their eyes to the consequences of the future—when they are not accountable to themselves or their families—when they focus on only their supposed short-term needs— then watch out! Big trouble lurks ahead.

Unfortunately, it seems that this is a common theme in our country today, with politicians, basketball coaches and parents not accepting responsibility for the leadership roles they are supposed to fulfill.

Nowadays a family can virtually be bankrupt and re-ceive new credit cards. Recently, listening to the car ra-dio en route to work, a commercial blasted, "You need CASH Now! You've got to have CASH Now!! Stop by any time, bringing proof of employment, and we'll give you cold hard CASH Nowww!!!" Every time I hear this commercial, it sounds like the devil calling me to do evil deeds! It's the voice of desperation, greed, instant grati-fication—all for a payday hangover. These cash-advance firms are the closest form of legalized loan sharking in the market today.

Our parents and grandparents always paid cash. They borrowed only to buy their homes. The first credit card appeared in the early 1960s in New York City—the Diners Club card, followed by American Express, and then a large co-op of bank branches that introduced Visa, by 2008 offering more than two billion cards. Today, car loans, residential mortgages, furniture loans, revolving credit and rolling credit card balances repre-sent the majority of debt load for most Baby Boomers. Credit card balances with high interest rates have be-come a way of life for many young people—enabling and encouraging money abuse rather than its smart, proactive use.

The acquisition of money can be accomplished in various ways—through education, experience and the choice of a profession that results in an income. Prudent management of money, given the harsh economic realities of the past few years, has become imperative for many families.

While most people believe proper investment management is all about earning money on their money, the most important money principle is *discipline*. Families should be practicing and proactively teaching their children to spend less money than they earn.

Good money skills can be taught as early as age five or six, with the job falling primarily on parents and secondarily on grandparents. Money skills can be taught and reinforced in the same manner as habits, such as picking up toys, hanging up clothes, and helping to load the dishwasher. As with any good habit, parents need to install learning through consistency, discipline and sometimes tough love.

Unfortunately, the track record of today's parents in this

area is poor. First, some facts about parents' financial literacy, from the President's Advisory Council on Financial Literacy 2008 Annual Report to the President:

In August 2007, the Networks Financial Institute, Indiana State University, found that just 28% of U.S. adults view their personal financial knowledge as "very good" or "excellent." National Foundation for Credit Counseling, for example, found that only 29% of respondents could say what the interest rate was on the credit card they use most often, even when given wide ranges (less than 10%, 10-15%, 15-20% or more than 20%) as options.

From Charles Schwab's 2008 "Parents & Money" survey: Only about one in three parents (34%) has taught their teens how to balance a checkbook, and even fewer (29%) have explained how credit card interest and fees work. More than two-thirds of parents (69%) admit to feeling less prepared to give their teens advice and guidance about investing than they do the "birds and the bees."

While investing is cited by almost half (49%) of parents as more important for today's youth to learn about than it was a generation ago, few are teaching their kids about it. Nearly all parents (97%) believe it's important to teach their teens to save and invest for retirement, and almost half (48%) worry that their kids won't start saving soon enough. Yet only 19% have taught their teens how to invest money to make it grow, and even fewer (14%) have taught them what a 401(k) plan is.

There are no curricula in our schools that teach these money skills. Therefore, the responsibility of education devolves to parents, who themselves often are in need of training.

Fortunately, there are resources available to help.

My wife and I employed a simple approach with our children when they reached 6 years old. Its foundation is the principle of saving first, spending second. We paid our children their respective ages weekly, starting at age 6 ($6), and raised their weekly pay each birthday until age 12 ($12). Then the second stage of the program began. We required our children to save $25 every two months, which was matched, dollar for dollar, by us and invested in a mutual fund. This is similar to a 401(k) matching program, available through most companies. Initial seed money of $500 was placed into the mutual fund to begin the program.

The remaining money after savings was available to our

children to spend on anything they desired, with the understanding that birthday/holiday gifts were their responsibility, along with the purchase of toys, games, food, treats and other items. We, of course, provided all the children's basic needs.

Our children regularly asked questions about how much money was needed to buy a particular toy or other item. Much hand-holding was necessary to help each child decide how to manage their money—to save up enough to buy a $14 LEGO kit for themselves or a $10 gift for their cousin's birthday. Almost immediately, most of the whining to convince us to buy something ceased. No temper tantrums to deal with!

After a couple early rounds of cultivating thoughtful money-handling behavior, our children began to experience the restraints of economic reality and assumed responsibility for small saving and spending decisions independently.

Time progressed, and we observed the same mature "activity" with them as teenagers and young adults in more subtle ways.

As I write this, our children are adults who bargain-shop

for clothes in the mall, returning home sometimes with no purchases. They patiently wait two weeks for a sale, or comparison-shop at another store where an item may be purchased for less. Budgeting discussions about major potential purchases are routine, along with inquiries about the best ways to save and invest for the future.

Certainly, teaching money skills to one's family members is never without occasional dilemmas. Not everything works out perfectly. However, every two months, as our children grew up, cash was given to us to invest in their mutual funds, and in October and November greater amounts were saved in anticipation of the expense of December holiday gifts.

Learning to manage one's money wisely and well has to start very early in life. A Lake Forest, Illinois, couple founded the Money Savvy Generation in 1999, after 20 years in the financial services field. Their goal: Help develop money skills for 6-to-12-year-old children. Susan Beacham became painfully aware of the difficulty many people have in grappling with the concept of personal financial management and in teaching necessary lessons to their children. She aspired to develop a program that could be taught in schools.

Changing the Conversation

Drawing on the age-old concept of the "piggy bank," she created the Money Savvy Pig.™ The Money Savvy Pig has four chambers—one for each of the money choices that children have when they earn or receive money: save, spend, donate or invest. The pig comes in four transparent colors with the choices spelled out right on its belly. For a nominal cost, the Money Savvy Pig may be purchased, along with a guide for parents and colorful stickers to apply to help the children visualize their money choices. Check out www.msgen.com for more information.

Another great source for developing money aptitude is the *Ultimate Kids' Money Book* (1998) by Neale S. Godfrey. It is most appropriate for children ages 8 to 12, and is a good book to add to the list of other books parents read to their children.

Okay—now that you've gotten your child to age 12, it's time to take the next step. At about age 12 or 13, your children are ready to be capitated. I'm not suggesting the guillotine (although you may have considered this method to deal with a tween!). *Capitate* in the medical profession means to make an agreement to provide a service for a fixed price. This is very common with doctors who provide Medicare services, where prices are dictated by federal and state governments.

The book *Capitate Your Kids* (2000) by Dr. John E. Whitcomb provides a model for parents to help their children take the next step towards financial independence.

Basically, a 12 year old is given a $200 monthly budget to buy his or her clothes and other non-essential items. Mom and Dad no longer provide the clothing needs. These responsibilities are picked up by the pre-teen. As we all know, clothing must be purchased for certain sports, when the snow flies, et cetera. So, it may be somewhat tricky, and some hand-holding may be necessary, to help pre-teens budget their clothing purchases. However, they ultimately answer for their clothing decisions.

Dr. Whitcomb's book goes on to suggest expanding children's responsibility to other expense categories—even to the point where one's adolescent is paying rent as a junior and senior in high school. Of course, children are paying their parents back money that is capitated to them monthly. Still, they can go through difficult times when they run out of money before their next monthly capitation. By the age of 16, they also receive an ATM/debit card and checking account to transact their expenses.

By following these stages of good, solid, teachable money habits, your high school or college student graduates into the world with the ability to gift, save, spend and invest wisely. They will know how to budget and live within their means. They will understand that credit cards should be used only as a transaction convenience and not as a source of financing.

The greatest common denominator among my widely diverse clientele: Most of them save first and spend second.

Families experiencing money difficulties today in all probability have not practiced this core principle. As a result, they spend much of their time stressed out and preoccupied with money problems—rather than focusing on more important family issues.

Help your children and grandchildren master these skills starting at an early age. You will then send them off into the world with confidence in dealing with financial matters.

Money is an integral part of our lives, but it should not define us. Our dream is to see our children face all of life's challenges and reach for all of its opportunities with a solid foundation along the way.

Do You Have the Right KASH?

Shortly after the famous golfer Ben Hogan won the 1948 United States Golf Open Championship, he was involved in a serious automobile accident—a head-on collision with a bus. Ben was driving with his wife. He threw his body in front of her to cushion the blow, thus taking the major force of the crash.

As the ambulance was taking Ben to the hospital, Mrs. Hogan asked the police officer at the accident site to help her pick up his golf clubs, which were strewn all over the road. The police officer expressed his doubt that Mr. Hogan would ever use the clubs again.

Ben was expected to die that day. Doctors were flown in from throughout the country to save his life. They did save his life, but informed Ben he would never walk again. Ben insisted the hospital staff install an exercise bar above his bed and place his golf clubs in the room, even though he could not move his arms!

One year to the day after the accident, Ben tied another great golfer, Sam Snead, in a golf tournament. Ben went on to win 54 more tournaments after his near-fatal accident.

Like many of us, Ben had KASH. KASH stands for Knowledge, Attitude, Skills and Habits. Ben had a vast knowledge of the game of golf, and had developed the skills and ultimately the habits he needed to play the game at a very high level. But it was his *attitude* that made him a great player.

When we consider hiring a new staff member, we first hire for *attitude*, and second for knowledge.

The skills and habits necessary to perform a job are always changing. Over the past three decades, there has been an ongoing, relentless and fundamental change taking place, brought about by the microchip and its inescapable effect of accelerating change in our lives.

Joseph Schumpeter, the Austrian economist, borrowed the phrase "creative destruction" to describe economic changes in a democracy. Creative destruction is the constant in the ongoing growth of a democratic free economy. As new technology and information change, so do the new growth industries that thereby push aside dated, status quo industries. It took two generations for the automobile to push out the horse and buggy, during which time buggy-whip manufacturers consolidated and eventually died out. Digital flat-screen LCD televisions have virtually overtaken the traditional cathode ray tube ones in a matter of three years. The pace of change has quickened.

In order for you to stay current and be productive and valuable to society, your KASH must also change.

The loss of U.S. manufacturing jobs represents another devastating change. These job losses have been accelerating over the past three decades, with more rapid loss in the past 10 years. Many reasons exist for the shrinking of our manufacturing base. The two main ones: the low labor costs outside the United States (and the resulting shifting of jobs), and new job creation in the service sector.

Many people believe this is a very troublesome trend that might lead the United States to rely on foreign countries for all of our manufactured goods. Yet in their 2008 book, *Reality Check*, authors Dennis Keegan and

David West revealed that the United States was still first in manufacturing output with $1.73 trillion, followed by Japan with $953 billion and China with $760 billion. They go on to write that the U.S. is now manufacturing high-end technical and intellectual-property-related goods requiring less skilled labor. This is an important subject, but not one that will be detailed here.

At this point, however, let's review some statistics on why the job market is changing. The Organisation for Economic Co-operation and Development ranks the U.S. secondary educational system (grades 7-12) at 18th in the world. This fact does not sit well with many Americans. Concerted efforts have been made by politicians at every level to improve our schools. Still, we will need to have major, fundamental changes in our system before we see these statistics improve.

That said, The Times Higher Education - QS World University Rankings for 2009 places the United States No. 1 in the world for post-secondary (college) education. In fact, 54 of the top 200 colleges in the world are in America. Foreign students represent 4% of undergraduates and 10% of graduate-level students.

If you think we are still educating the "best and brightest" from throughout the world, you are correct. These best and brightest are not all going back home to work. Just one example: Dinesh D'Souza, an Indian-born prolific writer who began attending Arizona State University at age 18—who later decided to remain in America because of the freedoms and enormous opportunities to work and raise his family here. D'Souza has published *The Virtue of Prosperity* (2000) and *What's So Great About America* (2002), both worthy of a read. He and many other foreign immigrants are staying in the United States to join our service sector. This, by the way, represents a huge brain drain from foreign countries—one of the reasons the U.S. continues to be the world's leading economy.

Life here in America and elsewhere has been changing at an ever-faster pace. So much so that we sometimes feel like the proverbial hamster on the treadwheel.

Take a look at a technology that began in the late 1800s: the phonograph, or more precisely, recorded sound. Let's say you graduated from a post-secondary school in the late 1800s and subsequently pursued a career in the recorded-sound industry. Nothing much changed over the following 50 years. A worker could have concentrated on the skills required to do the job, worked diligently for 40 years, and then retired with the traditional gold watch.

Fast forward to a high school student pursuing a technical degree in the recorded-sound industry in 1970. A new gadget was about to hit the stores, called the eight-track cassette player. This student supposedly knows how life works. Granddad taught him a great work ethic, advised him to work hard and keep his nose clean— and he, too, could retire with a gold watch. Our young protégé jumps in with both feet, learns everything there is to learn about the eight-track cassette player, and becomes an expert.

Lo and behold, the 1980s roll around, the eight-track player goes the way of the dodo bird, and our young student jumps with both feet into the new cassette-player industry, thinking this is where he missed the boat the first time around. He goes to night school while he moves up the cassette-player corporate ladder to greater benefits and more opportunities.

In 2001, he is let go in a third wave of corporate downsizing, due to the loss of market share to the new recorded-sound medium, the compact disc (CD). He had watched the manufacturing plants close one by one in the '80s and '90s, with the remaining cassette players being manufactured in China. He watched one colleague after another downsized out of what were once extremely promising careers. Finally, even he, the hardworking, smart and efficient manager, is let go in the latest round of contractions.

He is now 52 years old, still loves the recorded-sound industry, but knows little about the new digital technology that defines the clear, crisp sound enjoyed when playing a CD.

The industrial model his father and grandpa lived under is long gone. The workplace is much different this time. The difference is time itself. Everything is moving faster—*feverishly* faster.

Let's examine these attributes of KASH one at a time. Knowledge is just that—what you know and can impart to others. In the service sector, we are paid for our knowledge. At the end of each work day, has your knowledge allowed you to bring value to others in the service you provide? One's pay is ultimately determined by how well we impart our knowledge to others and, in the process, benefit their daily lives. This knowledge can be employed by flipping hamburgers, helping a consumer on an 800 service call, producing an Excel spreadsheet, selling real estate, teaching our children, and a myriad of other service-industry positions.

If one's knowledge is analog technology and all the new products are digital, then go to China. In China, they use all of our cast-off analog equipment.

If China is not your cup of tea, then seek and gain new knowledge in another sector. One of the fastest-growing U.S. industries is adult education. *No surprise here!*

In 1908, a young reporter had the pleasure of interviewing Andrew Carnegie. Toward the end of the interview, Mr. Carnegie suggested he consider interviewing all of Carnegie's business acquaintances about how they became successful. Carnegie knew that if this young man were up for the challenge, he would learn what made these successful people tick. Over the following 20 years, Napoleon Hill interviewed 500 successful inventors, authors and business people, resulting in Hill publishing *Think and Grow Rich* in 1937. Since then, over 30 million copies of the book have been sold.

Napoleon Hill identified key attributes present in these successful people. One essential factor for this distinguished group was maintaining a constant positive attitude. Another—focusing on their primary purpose. Over time, Hill himself evolved into a more successful writer and businessman as a result of his 20 years of research.

A consistent strong purpose and positive attitude can lead directly to successful achievement in whatever path one chooses.

Skills and habits go together. Actually, there is one word that covers both: *discipline*. Many people believe discipline to be rigid, non-creative, difficult and boring. Actually, all of us—to a greater or lesser degree—possess and gladly rely on our discipline (our skills and habits).

To be sure, there is some confusion about just what a "habit" is.

You may have read or heard that a habit takes 14 days to learn. This is terribly misleading! A habit takes 14 days to learn, but two full years to KNOW.

On January 2nd of each year, U.S. health clubs are bustling with people, many of whom have made a New Year's resolution to exercise more and lose weight. By mid-February, the crowds are gone and the regulars— you know, those "disciplined" people—are still there doing their exercises routinely. Why? Because the regulars have been performing this habit for at least two years. It is deeply imbedded in their subconscious, making exercise automatic.

I had a huge surprise some years ago when my daughter started to drive, with my car insurance going up $1,200. The insurance companies know which drivers have *learned* habits and which have *knowing* habits. Teenagers have to "think" about pressing the long skinny pedal or the fat horizontal pedal.

We can't speed up this "knowing" process. If we acquire new skills and do those things necessary to turn them into knowing habits, it still will be two years before these skills become ingrained, real and lasting.

If you find yourself in a no-win position where an industry is downsizing, being re-engineered or re-organized, you eventually will be handed your pink slip. So you must re-set and begin a new learn/know cycle. Your livelihood protection depends on the amount of KASH you possess. KASH may require re-education—learning new skills and habits, while retaining a great attitude.

Many, many qualified people are always on the street, searching for jobs in industries that are contracting and dying. It is vitally important for you to look toward the future and go where the jobs will be.

All of us need to be continually educating ourselves so that we are acquiring new knowledge, and thereby can apply new skills and habits to the changing landscape of the global workplace. Perpetual self-renewal is also a survivor skill important to master in order to live a full, fruitful life actively employed in a job you love.

Life is about constant learning and growth using KASH as our guidepost.

I believe author and pastor Charles Swindoll said it best with his comment about *attitude*:

"The longer I live, the more I realize the impact of attitude on life. Attitude, to me, is more important than the facts. It is more important than the past, than education, than money, than circumstances, than failures, than successes, than what other people think or say or do. It is more important than appearance, giftedness, or skill. It will make or break a company...a church...a home. The remarkable thing is we have a choice everyday regarding the attitude we will embrace for that day. We cannot change the inevitable. The only thing we can do is play on the one string we have, and that is our attitude....I am convinced that life is 10% what happens to me and 90% how I react."

The Moment Is Now

I sat on a rock, overlooking the Cantwell Glacier in the Alaskan Range. I was 24 years old, just beginning my military career. My superior and I had hiked two days across two glaciers to this remote Bureau of Land Management cabin.

The small A-frame had been air-lifted here a decade earlier. Inside was a journal, chronicling fascinating stories by cross-country skiers and hikers over the past 10 years.

Our goal: To climb the mountain behind the cabin and then hike out 20 miles to the nearest road. But we were forced to stay put due to threatening weather. Disappointed by the forced delay, I decided to read a paperback left behind from a previous traveler.

As I sat on the rock reading, a movement across the glacier caught my eye. A very large serac (block of ice) fell from an icefall a few miles away. Suddenly, there was an explosive sound, resembling a loud thunderclap. I was awestruck. This serac had produced a deafening noise, but appeared as only a tiny blemish on the massive icefall that fed toward the 15-mile-long, 2,500-foot-thick glacier. The Tlingit native people, I learned later, describe this roaring sound as "white thunder."

It was a cosmic moment. I felt very small and insignificant in terms of the universe. Rarely since have I been able to recapture this feeling—the overwhelming sense of nature's beauty and incredible power.

Many of us have had similar experiences, whether staring into the angelic face of a newborn child or enjoying the peace and serenity of a magnificent sunset. These are emotional moments when time seems to stand still. They can be life changing.

What is important to you? The answer most likely is as different to each one of us as the six billion others on this planet.

The point is—this is a personal question. There is no manual; no set of absolute rules will help you or me determine what we should do day-to-day. However, there are a few guidelines that can help us pick a path that may eventually bring great happiness and fulfillment.

First and foremost—we need to set our brain in motion. Our brain is engaged and powered by electrical currents; there must be a negative and a positive pole or nothing happens. We can't initiate any action if we can't "see" in our mind's eye a representation of a good or a bad outcome. There is nothing for our brain to grasp if we are unable to paint a picture of the future we want.

Of course, the future never turns out quite like we planned, but it is very important to create tension—positive, exciting tension.

Without a clear picture of the future, we *procrastinate*.

As my mother used to say, an idle mind is the devil's workshop (we were never idle if my mother had anything to say about it!). Procrastination is a deadly enemy, keeping us from what we can be or do in this world.

Do you remember the first day of high school? It was scary. No more carefree, innocent grade school days. I clearly remember that first day, and who I met for the first time. As I carefully made my way down the hall among some very imposing upperclassman, another fellow newbie barreled toward me with great confidence, followed by a few friends.

Soon I got to know Terry personally and heard his "future story" various times over the next four years. Terry's story was always the same. He was going to be a politician and an influential one as well. Terry was elected our Student Council President, and after high school he eventually graduated with a law degree from Georgetown University. He worked his way up through the Washington political ladder and eventually met a state governor who decided to run for president of the United States. Terry McAuliffe raised funds for Bill Clinton's first and second presidential campaigns. Terry headed the Democratic National Committee (DNC) from 2001 to 2005 and chaired the Hillary Clinton for President Committee.

At 14 years of age, Terry knew exactly what he wanted. He knew what was important to him. He clearly communicated his future goal and ultimately was successful. I'm certain he did not plan from the beginning to head the DNC, but he certainly stimulated the necessary positive synapses in his brain to achieve a successful political future.

Our brain helps us attend to what is important by focusing our attention on the future. But is that enough? What about the incremental steps we need to take to get where we want to go? How do we distinguish day-to-day what is important—that is, what we should and should not spend time doing?

One of the biggest traps is busy-work, those relatively simple chores and easy tasks that keep us from the tougher stuff. —Hence the saying, "Nero fiddled while Rome burned."

We can easily be sidetracked by mundane tasks, ignoring the more important. Staying focused and on task is not easy. Technological distractions such as cell phones and e-mail don't help matters either. It's a wonder we ever get anything done!

My good friend and business partner, Ed Kelly, has twice completed the *Marathon Des Sables*, a.k.a. the "toughest footrace on the planet." This six-day ultra marathon is held in Morocco's Sahara Desert each April. Competitors are required to carry a backpack with a week's worth of food. The event organizers provide water and tents along the arduous 150-mile route. Temperatures can reach 115 degrees Fahrenheit, and the competitors complete the equivalent of six marathons in six days.

That's right—*six marathons*. One of the legs is a 55-mile course and typically takes all day and most of the night to complete.

Ed and his fellow competitors will tell you that it is both a physical and spiritual journey. In fact, the spiritual part is really why many competitors return each year.

The preparation is grueling. Competitors start training a year in advance, running for hours and hours, testing the limits of their endurance. Are they focused? Yes. Have they painted a picture of a good and poor result? Yes. Do they know what is important each and every day? Absolutely yes.

Running six marathons in the desert may not be your idea of fun, but it has captured Ed's imagination and challenged him. For six days, in a hot, arid desert of occasional sandstorms and surprise fauna encounters, he is completely transfixed on what he needs to do. For six days he is undeniably intent on what he must do and not do in order to reach the finish line.

Each day is a different kind of marathon. There's always a finish line to cross.

Here are some tips to help you focus and concentrate. First, only try to accomplish three things each day, five if you are very motivated. We're just not effective if we try to focus on more than three action items.

For those of you who are list writers, when was the last time you completed an entire list? Probably never. You probably do what most people do—transfer the items from your current list to a new list.

When I say three items, I don't simply mean do the dishes, take out the trash, and go to the grocery store. These are all necessary and important tasks but fall into the busy-work category. —Nothing exciting or stimulating here.

The big question—how to focus on what is important?

Over the past 10 years, there is one question I ask everyone I meet. "If we were meeting here three years from today, and we were to look back over those three years to today, what has to have happened during that period, both personally and professionally, for you to feel happy with your progress?"

My follow-up questions relate to dangers that must be overcome, strengths that can get the job done, and opportunities that are possible.

Changing the Conversation

Dan Sullivan, founder of Strategic Coach®, has mentored thousands of entrepreneurs, using The Strategic Coach Program™ to help them along the path to the next level of career growth. He created The D.O.S. Conversation™ to open doors to new opportunities, and asks The Dan Sullivan Question™ to help transform people's future.

The Dan Sullivan Question stumps most people. —Because it asks them to envision a picture of their future. The purpose? To help people achieve clarity, to simplify and prioritize, to evolve a personal framework of reference, and move forward.

Now, as the saying goes, Rome wasn't built in a day. To reach a future destination, one needs intermediate goals along the way. And that's Dan Sullivan's point. You must first build a picture of the future in your mind—then break it down.

All successful people have a vision of where they're going and some practical way to measure their progress along the way.

How do ultra marathoners prepare for Morocco's *Marathon Des Sables?* By systematically assembling a year, then a quarter, then a week and finally a daily schedule.

Sir Edmond Hillary, a poor sheepherder from New Zealand, and his Sherpa guide, Tenzing Norgay, reached the top of Mt. Everest on May 29, 1953. Hillary became interested in climbing at the age of 16 while on a school field trip. He was a gawky teenager and not very athletic, but upon returning from his World War II service, he decided to be the first person to climb Mount Everest.

You may be surprised to know that his first two attempts to scale the world's tallest mountain ended in failure. Yet with little money and a grand vision he ultimately succeeded.

Take inspiration from Sir Hillary's example. Pick a horizon and go for it. Visualize a worthy goal and determine what will help you attain it. Your own thing may not be to climb through the magical land of the snow leopard and the *yeti* to the oxygen-deprived heights at the Roof of the World. So be it. Happiness and fulfillment can be achieved many ways. It may be simply enjoying the peacefulness of nature, spending quality time with family and friends.

Whatever you do, experience the *awe*.

It can be life changing.

How the Brain Learns

Having a great attitude—becoming very knowledgeable and educated—is only the beginning of any life journey. The most important question we must ask ourselves is, "Where am I going?" What is the ultimate destination and what are the way stations along the route?

Understanding how our brain works is crucial to obtaining success in life. Success, of course, is defined differently by all six billion-plus people on our planet. It is why each one of us is an experiment of one.

When I was 11 years old in upstate New York, my cousin lived across the street. He told me he was going to join the band at our grammar school and play the trumpet. This sounded like fun. I immediately responded I would play the trombone. With my cajoling and constant insistence, my mom agreed to buy me a secondhand trombone for $105 that I would repay out of my paper route profits.

I still vividly recall walking into my first lesson with my "new" trombone in hand. The band teacher was an Italian immigrant who spoke broken English. He first demonstrated how to purse our lips and blow while allowing our lips to vibrate, to coax the first crude notes from our brass instruments.

Well, I tried for a half hour to emit one solitary sound from my trombone, with zero success. All that resulted was the sound of blowing air. As the band teacher circulated among the new students, checking their progress, he came upon me turning ever redder from blowing so hard. As he gave me individual instruction, I set down the trombone. My response to his instruction was, "I can't."

Before this utterance was barely out of my mouth, my band teacher became extremely angry. You would have thought I was an immigration agent denying him entrance into America. Very clearly, as I remember, he said, "You can't make music with this instrument until you say 'I can.'"

This puzzled me because I truly felt that there was no possible way to cause any sound to emerge from this contraption sitting in my lap. He made me repeat over and over, "I *can* purse my lips and blow through the trombone."

He then gave me a short lecture on how nothing is ever accomplished by saying "I can't." He assured me I would be able to make music if only I said "*I can.*"

You may have guessed the rest. As soon as I tried again, I blew my first note. It startled me as much as it startled him. The power of the brain took over and enabled an accomplishment where there was perceived failure.

Our brain is really three brains: the brain stem or "lizard" brain; the amygdala or "mammalian" brain; and the neo-cortex, otherwise known as the "human" brain. The neo-cortex is where we think. Generally we can divide the activity we generate while thinking into conscious or subconscious thought. The conscious represents about 15% of our brain power. The subconscious takes up the remaining 85%.

This may seem somewhat counterintuitive. We live the majority of our lives in a conscious state. We only seem to be in contact with our subconscious when we sleep. Trying to interpret our nightly dreams is difficult. But this is not the subconscious to which I'm alluding. Rather, it is the powerful mental engine that allows us to accomplish so much, and that allowed me to "play" the trombone.

Experiments have been conducted that illustrate the power of the subconscious. In one such experiment, two groups of people were asked to complete a simple exercise. They were given three minutes to draw a line between a larger five-pointed star superimposed over a smaller five-pointed star, where the space between the stars' respective outlines was uniformly almost a quarter-inch wide (see diagram). However, there was a twist. The subjects had to perform this task while viewing the

superimposed stars from a mirror image. There was no direct line of sight. They could only view the stars through the mirror, producing the effect of seeing everything in reverse and backward.

Try reading words from a T-shirt in front of a mirror. *Very difficult!*

Each person on the two teams spent an awkward, frustrating time trying to operate the small motor muscles in the hand with little success over the three-minute timed experiment. In fact, the resulting scribbling appeared to be the drawing of a two year old.

The second half of the experiment brought the first group back to the stars in the mirror image, following five minutes of "mental rest." Results were better the second time, but the scribbling now resembled the drawing of a five year old.

The second group went out and played basketball for a full hour. Then they returned to the experiment. They flawlessly stayed within the space between the two stars, completing the experiment in one minute—almost as competent in their outlining as if they were looking directly at the superimposed stars.

So what happened? When we task our brain to solve a problem, the subconscious will work on it for a long time after our conscious mind has turned to other activities. Our subconscious actually continues to work out a solution!

Have you ever forgotten the name of an actor in a movie? The name of someone you met in the past? This happens to all of us. We say to ourselves, "I'll remember her name in a minute," or "It will come to me," or "I will recall it as soon as we get off the phone." What happens is, your subconscious works on the name while you consciously go about your business with your attention focused on other things. Then all of a sudden, out of nowhere, the name pops up in your mind. You virtually erupt with the answer to your query. Immediately you dial the phone and update your friend: "Humphrey Bogart in 'Casablanca.'"

Our subconscious constantly works on our various "interests."

Ever buy a new car and, for the next several weeks, all you see on the road is the make and model of your new car? The subconscious is highly tuned in with this new interest. When a young woman is pregnant, she may feel like she is surrounded by pregnant women. A friend confides in you about a rare medical problem, and the following day you see a newspaper article describing the disease. You're in a crowded restaurant, and your attention is suddenly pulled away from your table conversation to a diner nearby who's talking about an important interest of yours. As you walk through a busy airport with a cacophony of public announcements going in one ear and out the other, all of a sudden, your name is announced on a loud speaker. Your subconscious startles you into consciousness that something important to you has just occurred. Your name was announced.

We have many interests, and these interests change over time. Much like a sentry on guard duty, your subconscious vigilantly continues to "listen" and "look" for your interests in your daily life.

So, how can you consciously make your subconscious pursue the interests that are most important to you?

Thomas Edison was one of the greatest inventors of all time. He invented the light bulb, phonograph and motion picture camera, to name but a few. Many evenings while relaxing at home, he would sit down in a comfortable chair. In order to stir his creative juices, he would then place a metal ball in each hand and hold the metal balls in a relaxed position over two metal plates on the floor. As soon as he dosed off to sleep, his hands would relax, releasing the balls, which would suddenly awaken him as they clanged onto the metal plates. On numerous occasions, he would awaken with a new idea to help develop one of his myriad projects. Edison understood very well that his subconscious mind could deliver ideas to his conscious mind more rapidly in that quick interval when he was transitioning from a waking state to a sleeping state.

Another inventor, Elias Howe, was dreaming one night in 1845. In his dream, cannibals were stewing him in a large black pot, while performing a ritual dance around the fire. When he looked more closely, Howe noticed at the metal tip of each spear was a small hole running through the shaft. The up-and-down motion of the spears and the hole stayed with him when he awoke. The idea of passing the thread through the needle close to the point—not at the other end—was a huge innovation in making high-speed mechanical sewing possible. The sewing industry was soon revolutionized.

It is true that 1% inspiration equals 99% perspiration.

In April 2004, Edward Bowden, Ph.D., senior research associate at Northwestern University, along with his team, pinpointed the exact spot in the brain where such epiphanies take place. They discovered that insightful solutions are the result of a different kind of problem-solving than the communication and logical approaches normally applied by the left brain. The researchers discovered that a small area on the brain's right side registered a sudden burst in electrical activity (measured through magnetic resonance imaging) about one-third of a second before the "Aha!" or "Eureka!" flash of revelation.

Changing the Conversation

Interesting how Edison, Howe and others had this one figured out a long time ago!

One of the mysteries or misunderstandings about conscious and subconscious thought is the notion of right and wrong. It's true that we consciously make decisions about right and wrong throughout our daily lives. It's not true, however, that the subconscious knows the difference.

Think of your brain as being separated into two distinct compartments. Now imagine a computer operator sitting in the narrow opening between the two, encoding into the subconscious all the data that are written, spoken or thought about by you. Each time you perform a skill or exhibit a trait, this item is punched on the keyboard and saved into the subconscious.

In other words, the subconscious does not know right from wrong. Rather, it knows only what the conscious tells it. This is a much different reality from what we previously tended to think about ourselves.

A common example of this misperception involves people who say they don't remember names. They seem to remember phone numbers, dates of birth, addresses, and many details about a variety of things. So how come they don't remember names?

I used to be one of those people. It probably started like this. You are a high school freshman; a pretty girl turns to you in class and asks you for help with a math question. She calls you by name and, embarrassingly, you must ask her name even though she introduced herself to you at the beginning of the school year. You respond, "I'm not good at remembering names" as an easy excuse for your memory snafu.

At that very moment, your tiny computer operator keys in "I'm not good at remembering names" into your subconscious. Initially, this is a tiny byte of memory. But after many years of repeating the same response, this input has turned into hardened steel. It is now almost impossible to correct this error in subconscious thought.

You can now imagine my response to anyone who says the words, "*I can't.*" My immediate response is, "You're right if you say 'I can't'—try saying 'I can' a half-dozen times and see what happens."

One of my clients, Fred, has continually surprised me by how he is able to make ends meet when there is not enough money to pay his bills. On more than a dozen occasions in the past 20 years, Fred has surprised me with his ability to generate money just when it is needed to meet a late bill payment. These are not small bills, but expenses ranging from $50,000 to $1 million. Somehow, someway he has "found" the money through his business or the shuffling of assets in a manner to convince his bankers to loan him money.

On one occasion, Fred convinced an investor in one of his new ventures to advance him $1 million on an idea that was not yet developed. The $1 million was exactly what was needed to satisfy his bankers to provide capital for Fred's newest project. Several years later, the idea turned a handsome profit and tripled the investor's return.

Fred knows how to use the power of his brain to come up with a way to solve or resolve his money issues. He's a master at pulling innovative solutions presumably out of thin air.

Your brain is a lot more powerful than you think it is. Edison, Howe—and Fred—understood that the real power of our brain is in that huge subconscious engine. In a June 19, 2009, Wall Street Journal article, "A Wondering Mind Heads Straight Toward Insight," Robert Lee Hotz describes the power of the daydreaming state of mind. The article begins with the scientific insights of Newton, Descartes, Einstein and Tesla—their ability to grasp novel theories of gravity, coordinate geometry, relativity and alternating current.

Each scientist was involved in an activity unrelated to their discovery, when their insight took place.

The development of more accurate and detailed studies of our brain over the past 10 years is yielding results different than previously postulated. Through the use of brain scanners and EEG sensors, doctors are recording a much higher level of brain activity when we daydream.

Psychologist Dr. Joydeep Bhattacharya of the University of London's Goldsmiths College has reported in the Journal of Cognitive Neuroscience that subjects who solved a problem through insight showed a pattern of high-frequency neural activity in the right frontal cortex up to eight seconds before the solution dawned on the subject.

"It's unsettling," says Dr. Bhattacharya. "The brain knows, but we don't."

Getting Started to Getting Started

Our brain—indeed, our life!—will wander aimlessly if we do not *definitize* what we want to accomplish, experience or transform.

The trick is using the power of our brain to set specific guidelines and envision very specific results.

We must create a tension between where we currently are and where we want to be.

The United States, arguably the freest democracy in the world, has the fewest roadblocks to success. We can be what we want to be, when we want to be—at any time, without threat of loss of life or property. More than half of the world's people do not have this freedom of choice, lacking a strong government and strong capital to back it up.

What does this signify? If we are honest with ourselves, we have no excuse not to succeed.

Shortly after earning my high school diploma, I read a Reader's Digest article about a newly released study involving a high school class that had graduated 30 years earlier. At the time of their commencement, students were asked what they planned to do with their lives, their goals, and where they saw themselves 30 years in the future. After three decades, the high school classmates assembled for a reunion, whereupon each individual's accomplishments were compared against the original goals.

Two students out of the class of 100 had accomplished their goals and actually surpassed them. The difference between these two and the other 98 was that the two students wrote down their goals. The other 98 expressed them verbally.

What is the secret behind learning to play a trombone in high school, or the key to success for high school graduates?

Why don't we all achieve the goals we express verbally or muse about in our minds?

It all boils down to the proper use of our brain. The setup is quite simple. Writing down goals is a powerful, proactive stimulus to our subconscious, allowing us to define our purpose and achieve our destination.

Goals engage the subconscious to work on what we have deemed important. They help us use our brains proactively to address important issues.

The first step: Commit your thoughts to paper. There's a wonderful connection between the conscious writing of a thought and the subconscious determination to focus on achieving a goal. When we write a goal, we etch an entry directly into the subconscious. We are actually "writing" on our brain. When the goal is revisited and edited, the connection to the subconscious is strengthened. Each time this occurs the subconscious focuses more intensely on how to reach and achieve the specific objective.

Goal-setting is not terribly difficult; we just need to do it. The majority of day-to-day life is "doing," not putting off until we are comfortably ready, and not waiting for others to help us do it. Installing goals is all about doing them—and doing them as soon as possible.

Nothing happens until someone takes action.

Inertia holds progress hostage.

For instance, you may want to achieve financial independence by completing a joint venture with a competitor that brings new products to market (opportunities), using your personal abilities (strengths) of persuasion and careful attention to details. In doing so, you also decrease your market competition and financial dependence (dangers). Your goal has provided the compass and coordinates to avoid dangers, employ your strengths, and pursue new opportunities.

Let us say you envision completing a marathon three years from now, during the month of your birthday, in a time under four-and-one-half hours. Your family waves at the finish line, cheering as you cross the line in four hours and 25 minutes, with time to spare. You feel very healthy, have lost 25 pounds, and are happy with the physiological and emotional balance in your life.

That is a specific goal. It is one that your brain can grasp onto and create the necessary tension to move you subconsciously onward to the finish line.

Actually, "getting started to getting started" is the hardest part. First visualizing the goal, then writing it down in specific terms, and finally sharing the goal with family and friends—that's where one's future begins.

A tall order? Hard to achieve? By no means—the key is to get started setting goals. If you want action, this works.

The next step is to break the goal down into one-year goals, three-month goals and, finally, goals over the next 30 days. A one-year goal might be to run a 10K race in one hour. A three-month goal might involve running one mile in 10 minutes. A 30-day goal might require logging 10 miles weekly for the next four weeks—running and walking on a track or treadmill, or in your neighborhood or local park. The 30-day goal is your to-do list. It is the habit you are attempting to form.

At the end of each 90-day period, you will again set the next 90-day goal, keeping in mind and reviewing the one-year and 30-day goals.

Timing is the only factor that affords you some wiggle room. You may elect to complete the marathon in two years or four years. The important point is, you have *definitized* and established a very clear objective to be accomplished within a specific guideline and time frame.

Let's go back for a moment. One of the reasons why

we are hesitant to write down goals is due to past nega-tive experience of not accomplishing them in the time allotted. One important item to remember is that most things in life are beyond our control. If a goal is to meet one's family for the holidays and a major snowstorm can-cels connecting flights, then it is very unlikely this goal will be achieved during this particular holiday season. It is okay for a goal to be postponed as long as we continue to strive forward.

I am in contact with many successful business owners who focus so closely on their specifics that they forget to give themselves any credit when they miss the year's sales target—even though their sales have increased 23%, just shy of their 25% target goal.

We are our own harshest critics. So, celebrate your ac-complishments. Remember—all of us miss 100% of the shots we don't take.

For a moment, consider envisioning yourself at 100 years old reflecting on all the things you have accom-plished, then write them down. Sounds absurd? Well, I once read a story about a man who wrote down 112 life-time goals when he was age 18 in the 1940s. These were major goals. By the early '70s, he completed 37 of them, and by the '80s, the number grew to 95. If he is still living, then possibly he has already attained all 112 goals.

An exercise you might consider involves writing down your 12 lifetime goals. Again, ask yourself The Dan Sullivan Question™. Many times, exercises are much easier to do with someone who knows you well: a spouse, colleague or close friend. Go through the process of establishing specific goals, writing them down so your brain activates and begins pursuing them. Start at building the Big Picture, then composing one-year goals, followed by 90-day goals and, finally, 30-day goals (the to-do list).

Unlike the acorn that grows into a tall oak tree under ideal botanical conditions, we as busy human gardeners continually plant a whole multitude of shrubs, flowers, trees, herbs and vegetables—each one germinating and growing on a different time schedule. Without a plan— without lifetime goals—our life's botany can quickly become unchecked, unmanageable, a chaotic jungle. This will result in much wasted effort and aimless lives.

Identifying and writing down a specific path through the underbrush is key to maintaining focus and charting a course to a happy life.

The last step is to try to accomplish something each day. Start with three things. If you accomplish just three things every day, your subconscious will continue to direct you toward your 30-day tasks. Don't try to do everything on your list each day. This will only end in disappointment. Always—*always!*—write down the three things to accomplish each day. Write them down the prior week or day, but no later than the first thing that morning. This one habit can spell the difference between a life of unfulfilled wandering and a life of constant positive growth.

In Peter F. Drucker's book *Managing in the Next Society* (2002), he took a long view of business over the next 30 years. As a prolific writer and lecturer, until his passing in 2005 at the age of 95, Drucker emphasized that successful managers must be highly focused and adaptive to today's unprecedented demographic, economic and sociological transformations. These include the "information revolution" and the new knowledge-worker society. His many insights continue to inspire those who seek future growth.

In golfing legend Arnold Palmer's office, Drucker once noticed, there is only one trophy: a battered little cup that Palmer got for his first professional win in the 1955 Canadian Open. There is also a single plaque that reads: "If you think you are beaten, you are. If you think you dare not, you don't. If you like to win but you think you can't, it's almost certain that you won't."

Life's battles don't always go to the stronger woman or man. But sooner or later, those who *win* are those who think they *can*.

It starts with the first step, and that step is much easier with written goals behind it.

Do the Correct Thing

When stationed with the U.S. Army in Fairbanks, Alaska, I spent a year with an air cavalry unit. Almost every day, we flew around in UH-IH "Huey" helicopters, the ones seen in Vietnam War footage.

On one particular mission, we flew from 2,000-foot elevation with a complement of troops and equipment to land at 7,000-foot elevation on the side of a mountain next to a glacier. Beforehand, we had performed a pre-flight check of the load to ensure the airframe would be stable at the higher altitude. But as we approached the landing zone, the helicopter started to exhibit signs of distress. At about 50 feet off the ground, we began to lose tail rotor control because the main rotor was too heavily loaded—apparently an error was made in our pre-flight check.

Not good.

Changing the Conversation

We began to spiral out of control and gyrate at 90-degree angles to the ground, which was only 30 feet away. Very scary! I thought at any moment we would die or be dismembered in a fiery crash. Miraculously, the aircraft righted itself at the last possible moment and landed hard on the ground. No one was hurt, except for everyone's very raw nerves and severe emotional distress.

The site was cordoned off awaiting the National Transportation Safety Board inspection. About 10 minutes after the crash, while I was calming my nerves and thanking God for our safe crash landing, the pilots walked over to me. I was the ranking officer on the crash site, so they approached me with a "situation."

They explained that they had forgotten to remove an open bottle of whiskey from their kit bag prior to stowing it on the aircraft. This was obviously a major violation that could end up with both of them being discharged from the U.S. Army without pension or benefits. The senior pilot had 19 years in and was scheduled to retire the following year. We were "in the field" so it was not unusual for the pilots to have alcohol in their tents for consumption between missions. The senior pilot had removed the bottle from the kit bag on the damaged helicopter and he now showed it to me inside the flap of his flight suit.

Suddenly all of those ethics lessons and training at West Point and my officer courses came crashing down on me. What do the regulations say? Were they drinking within 12 hours of starting their mission? When reported, what are the ramifications to them and me? What would their flight commander do if he was here? He was my boss as well.

Before I reveal the outcome of this ethical dilemma, some background: The United States military spends a lot of time preparing their officers and non-commissioned officers for ethical situations. Why? Because men and women will be put in harm's way, meaning it is a matter of life and death.

When I began attending honor code and ethics classes at West Point, it did not go very well for me. I hated being put into situations where there were no good solutions. I didn't like to be placed into gray-area decision-making, and I distinctly remember one particular ethics scenario: "You are an escaped prisoner of war behind enemy lines making your way back to friendly lines. You are injured and the enemy will catch you before you are able to make contact with friendly forces. You are at a local watering hole used by a small village of some 25 people. Your pursuers will track you to this watering hole and refresh themselves as you are doing right now. You have tablets that can be used to poison the water, killing anyone who should drink from the watering hole over the next 24 hours. What do you do?"

To a young fire-and-guts 19 year old, this was not fair. I don't want to be captured nor do I want to kill innocent civilians. This is one of those "no win" situations… or is it?

This classroom exercise was designed to help a young officer deal with ambiguity and reason through to the correct solution; in other words, do the right thing.

The turning point for me in my ethics education was this particular exercise, because I had to measure three sets of lives: mine, my pursuers, and 25 innocent civilians. The answer was simple, or was it? Was the right thing to poison the watering hole, knowing the enemy may arrive first, drink the water and die at the watering hole, alerting the civilians to the tainted water? Was the right thing to move on and hope to make it to friendly lines before being captured? No one can really know how they will confront such a decision, unless they are on the ground experiencing the specific situation in the immediate moment. We just don't know how we will react when the "bullets are flying." Each of us has a very strong survival instinct. It is hard to say what we would do. But—back to Alaska.

Okay. Lieutenant, what do you do? This is the real deal. It is not life or death, mind you, but several careers could be ruined, including mine. Neither of the pilots had alcohol on his breath. They appeared in a quandary and I believed their explanation.

I decided to take the bottle, toss it over my shoulder to the rocks and glacier below, where it shattered into a thousand pieces, leaving no evidence.

A scary time for the second time within 10 minutes! I informed the pilots we would meet with our boss upon returning from the field in a few days, relay this part of the story to him, and accept any consequences due to our actions.

Fortunately, he agreed with my decision. He then put the two pilots on every lousy, awful weekend and holiday duty available until their departure from Alaska.

Right or wrong? I felt like it was the right thing then, and I still feel I did the right thing, 25 years later.

I'm a black-and-white type of guy, so, like many of you, the ethical decisions we make during our lives are difficult. Through the school of hard knocks we get bumped and bruised along the way. Hopefully we don't wreak too much havoc.

When we help our clients deal with money decisions, the gray areas seem to widen. Sometimes, legal and regulatory ambiguities create complexity. But oft times—not.

Do we act on insider information? Do we cheat on our taxes? Do we hide assets from the government to reduce onerous estate taxes at death? These involve straightforward rights and wrongs.

The really tough situations tend to be dealing with others, especially our family. How do we handle a son and daughter-in-law who are spending beyond their needs, constantly asking us for financial help? Maybe it is okay to buy an airline ticket home or send a couple thousand dollars to pay for an unexpected home-repair expense. But it may not be long before we are giving them $30,000 to $40,000 annually, while they spend beyond their means or even cut back their work hours to spend more time at home. Maybe this is legitimate because there are young grandchildren to raise. Or maybe not. These are really tough situations. We may be enabling them while continuing to fuel their desire for more money without any kind of restraint.

Dealing with our loved ones and our friends when it comes to money is difficult at best. It does eventually work out if we take the time to review each situation, address the ambiguity, and make the right decision.

Sometimes it is difficult to see what is the right thing to do.

A few years after leaving Alaska I found myself in the famed 82nd Airborne Division at Fort Bragg, North Carolina— an elite unit ready to go to war within 12-hours notice. Nicknamed "America's Guard of Honor," it is air transportable, airborne, light and fast.

I worked on the division staff for a colonel with nine other fellow captains. One day, a co-worker came to me with a "situation." He had noticed and verified that our boss had signed a document showing that he had jumped that prior Saturday with the Sport Parachute

Team. My co-worker knew, in fact, that our boss had convinced one of the team members to lie for him, corroborating his fictitious jump.

At that time we were required to make parachute jumps every three months in order to collect our $110-per-month jump pay. The colonel was exhibiting other problems as well. He had been observed cheating on his wife and had gone so far as to have several of us drop him off at his mistress's home during the work day. This comes under the "conduct not becoming an officer" in military regulations. There were other frustrating professional infractions as well. The colonel was a highly decorated, three-tours-in-Vietnam war hero. In hindsight, it is obvious that he was going through some kind of mid-life crisis. He was self-destructing before our very eyes.

So, what did we do?

Each of us 10 captains wrote up depositions itemizing every infraction we had each experienced and submitted them to the commanding general. The colonel was brought in front of the general, read his rights, dismissed from his position, and brought up on charges to be tried in a court-martial under military law.

At the time, we felt like we had done the right thing. Still—there was a part of me during that episode that I unfortunately didn't listen to, which I should have minded. We were so busy with our righteous pursuit of a miscarriage of justice that we paid no attention to the colonel's cues for help. He needed a counselor, a break in duty, an advocate to straighten him out. But we offered him no quarter.

About six months later, after 19.5 years of service, he was dismissed from the U.S. Army with no benefits and no pension. He did not deserve this. We did the right thing pursuant to military regulations, but we missed the "higher" right because we were too busy taking the high ground on our righteous horse. We missed the mark completely.

Frankly I have replayed these events in my mind various times over the last 25 years, wondering how I and nine other captains missed the obvious problem to be addressed.

A professor in an ethics class I attended while studying for my master's degree provided me with a great insight into wise decision-making. During class we spent two hours role-playing a difficult client scenario that at times created very heated debate. The majority of the class was at odds with one classmate who had taken the "other side."

It was a setup of sorts—the case study wasn't about rules, regulations and the right decision based on the facts. The professor opined that in many situations there is the right answer and then maybe a "higher right" answer. Looking back, I had experienced this "higher right" with the helicopter pilots, but had failed to identify the "higher right" in providing help to the self-destructing colonel.

In life, one faces daily conundrums involving right and wrong as well as good and bad. Over my lifetime, squaring regulatory orders and "rightness" with ethics and individual "goodness" has posed the greatest challenge and also afforded the opportunity for greatest satisfaction.

The inspiration for this conversation came from watching a recent Hollywood movie release, "Gone Baby Gone." In the movie, Casey Affleck is a young private detective who is searching for a three-year-old kidnapped girl. The girl's mother prostitutes herself for drugs and alcohol. As one eventually learns, the mother's brother had decided to team up with a police captain who had lost his own 12-year-old daughter in a senseless murder years earlier to kidnap this girl from the mother's apartment.

In the movie, the police captain sets up the kidnapping scene as if some no-good pedophile or twisted crook had made off with the girl. Eventually, about five people die along the way as the private detective reveals more and more of the plot. Those who die are linked directly back to the "righteous" kidnapping.

Near the end of the movie, Casey Affleck stands across from Morgan Freeman, the police captain, who is holding the young girl. The girl now has Morgan and his wife raising her in a beautiful suburban home far from the dirty streets of South Boston. She is far from her mother, who makes terrible parenting decisions—safe from the horrible world. Don't we all want this for our children or grandchildren? You bet we do! And that is the crux of the story. Detective Casey Affleck has a right vs. wrong, good vs. bad decision to make:

Don't report the kidnapping that only he is aware of, or report it and return the daughter to her misfit mother. Morgan Freeman and his wife will be sent to jail, along with the mother's brother.

Casey decides that the right/good thing to do is return the daughter to the mother. Why? Because a wrong/bad thing started this tremendous mess. The kidnappers could have easily contacted Child Services and had the girl's uncle granted custody, resulting in him raising the niece.

Obviously, this movie made a profound point—a huge slippery slope here! Many right and noble intentions after a wrong decision do not override the wrong committed.

Doing the correct thing is what defines who we are.

As we plan our estates and work to preserve them for our children and grandchildren, we hope that we have provided them also with a foundation for ethical decision-making to guide them in their lives.

It is the legacy we leave.

All the money and material possessions we pass on pale by comparison to what we stand for and how we conduct our life. Making right and good decisions at many times is very difficult and we don't always succeed. But our choices—properly made—will lead to positive life-changing events, rippling out to affect many others we touch during our lives.

The Psychology of Money

Money talk is tricky business.

You just don't know who to trust or how your money will be perceived by others, even close family members.

The following story demonstrates. Some years back, my 5th grade daughter asked, "Are we rich?" She asked this question because a classmate had assumed this to be true, and her parents noted that we lived in a large home.

The question exposed a reality that needed to be acknowledged and discussed in a meaningful way. It was time to talk about values, both personal and financial. We acknowledged that we did have a nice home, nicer than most. We then pointed out that our good fortune was largely due to our hard work. We felt this was a real family teaching moment, but in reality, our daughter only wanted a yes or no answer. Herein lies the conundrum.

Comprehensive, meaningful money talk is as much a subjective exercise as it is objective. It is not just about numbers. It is also about the feelings, values and attitudes that reflect what we think and do regarding money.

But, as the story above illustrates, most don't readily perceive money in terms of values. The question then is, what can we do about this? How can we impact our children's attitudes—their psychology of money, if you will?

I suggest that financial literacy is the first step.

What is financial literacy? Consider this definition taken from a study: "Personal financial literacy is the ability to read, analyze, manage and communicate about the personal financial conditions that affect material well-being. It includes the ability to discern financial choices, discuss money and financial issues without (or despite) discomfort, plan for the future, and respond competently to life's events that affect everyday financial decisions, including events in the general economy" (Journal of Financial Service Professionals, November 2004).

Now, let's look at some statistics regarding U.S. financial literacy. The 2008 annual back-to-school survey from Capital One found that only 14% of teens have taken a personal finance class in school. Some 69% of teens say that what they know about managing money, they learned from their parents. About 54% have not discussed the difference between "needs" vs. "wants." Half of teens (50%) expressed an interest in learning more about managing money, and 76% say they want to learn about the basics of finance because it will help them make better financial decisions down the road.

The 2008 Financial Literacy Survey of adults, conducted on behalf of the National Foundation for Credit Counseling, Inc., and MSN Money, revealed: Only 59% of the young adults in Generation Y (ages 18-29) pay their bills on time every month. According to a 2008 survey by The Hartford Financial Services Group, Inc.: 55% of parents with children aged 16-24 voiced concern over their children's ability to become financially independent without monetary assistance from them.

In 2008 the savings rate in the United States was under 1%. This very low savings rate, coupled with subprime mortgages, resulted in many people being forced to abandon their homes and declare bankruptcy. —All because they did not understand that their mortgage interest rate could adjust up causing significant, negative personal cash flow.

This scenario becomes even more dismal as corporations continue to terminate the funding of defined benefit plans, which pay out a monthly pension upon retirement.

Over the past 30 years, there has been a gradual shift toward employees being responsible for funding their own retirements through 401(k) plans. Many of those who retired in the 1960s, '70s or '80s did not have to be concerned with or understand the stock market. Upon retirement, they received monthly pension checks from their employers. Their employers managed large stock and bond portfolios to meet the requirements of their pension payouts.

Things have changed. Today's 21st century workers now need to understand how to invest their 401(k)s in the stock and bond fund investment choices provided by their company. But good, solid money decisions about financial products and strategies require personal finance literacy. Unfortunately, our schools do not provide this education.

Financial literacy happens when financial education is coupled with a desire to learn and apply sound financial concepts. This becomes problematic when money decisions are subverted by emotion. Professional marketers understand and use human psychology to their advantage. Credit card commercials may list itemized costs— but entice with references to love, memories, relationships, and the punch line "priceless." We are coaxed to buy, based on a seductive appeal for things that we covet. This is how we get into trouble.

Without firm dedication to financial literacy standards, we tend to rationalize spending decisions, not considering the financial consequences. Let's look at an example.

You have been driving a minivan to ferry the kids around for the past 10 years and now it's time to buy a real car. Great, it's time to go car shopping! You know you can afford a car in the $25,000-$30,000 range, equating to car or lease payments of $350 per month. The current van you drive is coming off lease at this same monthly cost, and money is tight. You visited Ford, GM and DaimlerChrysler dealerships, have plenty of reasonable choices—but the luring voice of unreason begs consideration as well.

Why? Your next-door neighbor just bought a Lexus. You would really like a Lexus. Who wouldn't? The Lexus experience! So, you drive to the nearest Lexus dealership and are taken in immediately. The cars are much nicer. There's espresso and child care. Their service bay floors are cleaner than your kitchen table. You are captivated! You test drive the new model, it purrs like a kitten, and has an orchestra sound system with every feature imaginable. You ask the price—a four-year lease for $750 per month.

Come on, you can handle that. There's a raise coming in the future, and if not, there is still $10,000 on the home equity line of credit to make up the shortfall. It's only an additional $400 per month.

Deep down, alarm bells are ringing. You are not really feeling comfortable. But the alarm is ignored. Heck, you deserve it (greed). Your neighbor has one (envy/jealousy). It will look great in the driveway (pride). You love all those wonderful features (lust). And so, good sense is dismissed. You sign the lease agreement and drive home in your brand-new Lexus.

I believe you just committed five of the seven deadly sins (sloth and wrath are the other two)—or as the 1970s comedian Flip Wilson's character, Geraldine, used to say: "The devil made me do it."

Because we are a consumer-based society, this scenario plays out over and over again. One would hope that when faced with these lease choices, we would make a value-based decision grounded on financial literacy, recognizing the danger of spending beyond our means. Such a rational understanding should lead us to buy the affordable car. But, as this story shows, we are typically not driven by rational understanding when it comes to money. Too often we are seduced down the wrong path, captive to our emotions. And if we take this seductive road too often, we become addicted.

Some simple tools can help ensure sound financial decision-making. It is beneficial to consider three important guidelines—*sufficiency, sustainability* and *appropriateness. Sufficiency* is about answering the question, "Do I have enough?" This is the first question we ask anytime we consider taking on a new expense or a new financial commitment. We ask this question when paying monthly bills, making large, one-time purchases, buying a first or second home, paying for a child or grandchild's college education, or taking a vacation.

The second important guideline is *sustainability*, "How long will my money last?" Pre-retirees often ask this question as they contemplate retirement. *Sustainability* requires that we be well-informed about our assets, cash flow and taxes. Without sufficient earnings from our assets, there may not be sufficient income to pay our ongoing expenses. Will you have enough slack in the rope to not have to fret over marginal purchases, or will you have to go without? Can you afford to travel, maintain two homes, or provide financial assistance to your grandchildren? Can you do all of this without depleting your assets? All spending decisions must be considered and balanced in light of *sustainability*.

A third financial decision-making guideline is *appropriateness*, or "How do I stay out of financial trouble?" You must always consider whether or not an expenditure, financial strategy or investment opportunity is appropriate for you. *Appropriateness* was an important consideration in our earlier car-buying story, and is certainly a key question when buying, say, a second home. This question is easily answered by those with surplus income who have already addressed sufficiency and sustainability. But sometimes a financial decision may pass the sufficiency and sustainability test, but fail to pass the *appropriateness* test. Buying a brand new car for a teenage daughter may not be appropriate if she has not learned to manage her finances. It may be more prudent to buy a safe, late-model, reasonably priced vehicle for her use.

In the 1996 movie, "Jerry Maguire," Cuba Gooding, Jr. keeps asking his agent Tom Cruise to "show me the money!" Throughout the course of the movie, these two men are transformed into different, happier, healthier people by learning not to focus on the money, but rather, taking care of each other.

Making good financial decisions and focusing on the truly important issues of the day allows money to play its proper supporting role, not the leading role.

Mine the Minds of Mentors

An old Eastern proverb suggests that "When the student is ready, the teacher appears."

At first glance, this statement might not seem that "earth shattering." After some thought, however, a crucial point becomes clear. One does not learn until one is ready to learn. We all have the ability to learn, but we often throw up roadblocks that prevent us from being open to new thoughts and ideas that stimulate new learning and development.

Mentoring is one way to keep "turning over the soil" in terms of ongoing development. What is a mentor? What role does this person serve in the management of our personal and financial affairs?

Well, for one thing, there are very few families who truly have their financial act together. America has many addictions: drugs, alcohol and even processed sugar (it's in 99% of everything we eat!). Our addiction to money probably comes close to the top of the list. We can do virtually nothing today without money. There is very little bartering, and we have disconnected ourselves from the origination of most goods and services.

We need each other and the world to continue our way of life.

Money mentorship is of vital importance at any level of wealth. While I don't try to dissuade people with true philanthropic objectives, I do try to get those with the "I'll spend it all" attitude to look at more practical and lasting solutions. Preparing their children for future roles as custodians of the wealth that they and their families may have accumulated is one of the most important solutions to their concerns.

Why mentoring? Recently I ran across a reference to the 33 greatest American entrepreneurs of the last 150 years. Among those represented were Carnegie, Edison and Rockefeller as well as Warren Buffett and Bill Gates. There were some interesting comparisons made among these entrepreneurs, which resulted in some core commonalities.

Having mentors, strong partners and associates topped the list. Some may believe that Thomas Edison was a lonely inventor whose research and contributions were solely a result of his own isolated efforts. In reality, he had a staff of 120 employees plus partnerships with some of the great entrepreneurs of his time. John D. Rockefeller, III, was mentored by his father John D. Rockefeller Jr. and now runs one of the most successful productive charitable foundations in America.

Mentoring happens in all directions, up, down and laterally. The classic mentor relationships from history were everyday leaders—people such as blacksmiths and coopers. Today we have apprentice programs for electricians, plumbers and carpenters, and intern programs for doctors, lawyers and accountants. Where these programs are in place, competent work or advice is expected and for large part delivered.

Still, a significant segment of our population isn't part of any structured mentorship program or involved in any mentor relationship. And many of those who are mentored early on or interned don't have a program after they reach their earning years. As a result, many people are struggling to develop themselves without any idea of where to start.

I've been fortunate to have three sets of great mentors over the past 35 years. The first was a high school teacher and coach, who encouraged me to consider attending West Point and then a career as a U.S. Army officer. There were two generals and two colonels whom I attempted to emulate while serving in the Army. My latest mentor has patiently worked with me over the past 20 years to shape me into a business owner, consultant and trusted advisor. The latter's influence also has helped me write with greater focus and frequency.

Some way, some how, mentors can impart their life lessons and experiences to us if we are only willing to be open to new ideas and new ways of approaching life.

Mentors are everywhere. They are parents, teachers, spouses, children, coaches, friends, community and religious teachers and leaders, and everyday people we meet throughout our lives.

They, however, cannot help us unless the passion to learn and change starts from within.

For the young, their parents temporarily cease to be mentors when they begin high school—often until sometime after they have their own bills to pay and family to support. Ironically, just when others in their lives are looking to them for guidance, their parents become smart again!

Mark Twain once quipped: "When I was a boy of 14, my father was so ignorant I could hardly stand to have the old man around. But when I got to be 21, I was astonished at how much the old man had learned in seven years."

Parents and grandparents watch from the sidelines, waiting for the moment when their children will emerge from their adult cocoons ready to really take on the world.

Recently I was chatting with my niece about her new job, asking how things were going. She said she disliked her boss and had come to realize at age 24 that she needed a mentor. She'd spent three years in the real job world after college, had experienced a lack of focus and the unhappiness that comes with having a difficult boss, and had no one to turn to for advice.

She's just looking for someone who will help her along, someone to counsel and guide her in making decisions about her life direction. She doesn't want to reinvent the wheel. She simply recognizes the advantage of having a good mentor who can measurably shorten the learning time.

And she's right. A well-chosen mentor is essential to her personal and professional development. Wise counsel now will help her produce greater results in her future—provided she stays humble, works diligently, and continues to clarify her goals.

I met with a prospective client a few years ago who just could not see the benefit of hiring a wealth counselor— that is, someone who will mentor, coach and advise him on important family and financial issues. He was nearly age 60 and still adamant about controlling, supervising and managing his assets.

The only problem was, he reviewed his affairs on such an infrequent basis that he never really addressed his current dangers or took advantage of sound opportunities. It was costing him in his portfolio.

This is the investor who invariably buys high, sells low. He has trouble detaching himself from prior poor decisions and can't "cut bait" and take his losses. This prevents him from keeping up with new ideas and further adapting to changing market, tax and business environments. He works full time and can't quite get around to reviewing his stuff—until after problems have taken root and he is forced to react desperately "once the damage is done."

Like so many people, he is focused on something myopic, like trading costs, administrative fees, owning the perfect stock, or making sure all the dividends hit his account.

Meanwhile, it's September 15, 2008. He has 90% of his entire life's savings in the stock market. When he finally takes action in January 2009, his portfolio is 50% of its value from when he bought those stocks. And, he has ignored other investment choices that now seem far more prudent.

I'm not saying that money details aren't important. They are. However, proper money management is critical and it really isn't that difficult. What my prospective client needs is a money *mentor*. —Someone to help advise him on the Big Picture stuff.

Over many years, I have found that successful people tend to be good decision-makers. What many of them are not good at is defining how to think about the money issue.

Good mentors help others get their arms around their

situation so that decisions can be made without losing any momentum.

As I said, mentoring works up, down and laterally. At our company, we have established a mentoring program. Every week, each staff member meets for one-half hour with usually a more experienced staff member. We have found that the supposed mentor may often glean as much or more in these sessions as the person they're supposed to be helping! We have found our mentoring program to be extremely helpful in maintaining open lines of communication within our office.

To those of you who are married, spouses can be tremendous sources of important mentoring. A few years ago I was reading a story about the early days of Henry Ford. Everyone thinks of Ford as a tough businessman, but he didn't start out that way. In the late 1890s when he was perfecting his internal combustion engine, he hit what he thought was a permanent impasse. He needed to make an engine modification that would cost him $45. When he sought to have the modification made, he asked that it be done on credit.

To his utter dismay and distress, no one would extend him the credit. He returned home dejected, in despair.

Sharing the bad news with his wife, he concluded that he had no alternative but to forego his dream and resign himself to a "regular job" with regular wages.

His wife abruptly stopped him in his tracks. She reminded Henry that she had saved up $60 as an emergency fund to help them through any lean times. She insisted he stop moping about with a defeatist attitude, take the $45, and make the necessary repairs to his engine.

A great piece of mentoring by Mrs. Ford—and the rest is history.

In *The Millionaire Next Door* (1996), authors Thomas J. Stanley, Ph.D. and William D. Danko, Ph.D. note that one of the most common characteristics of these millionaires is a long-term marriage with an average of three children.

There is something to be said about the support that is received from mentor spouses.

And count yourself fortunate if you find yourself surrounded by young people. For them, life has no limits. They haven't gotten smart enough to know what can't be done. They're not yet infected with "the curse of knowledge"—the inability to see the forest for the trees.

The young embrace new technology and all the benefits that it brings to our lives. They're more willing to change since they have only themselves to answer to.

On the other hand, young people often make rash decisions and careless mistakes, some of which they have to live with for the rest of their lives. Everyone—including young people—are in desperate need of mentors.

None of us should ever take our mentoring duties lightly.

And always have the right someone mentoring you.

Are You a Chief or Indian?

During my 30-plus years in the workforce, I have met many memorable people. When I left the U.S. Army and started working at a Fortune 500 company, I met one particular co-worker who, to this day, sticks out clearly in my mind.

Bob worked with me in the management information system (MIS) department and was in his late 50s. He had seen many changes in MIS over the years, from computers occupying rooms the size of city blocks to the much newer 512-megabyte platter-type disc drives that occupied a filing-cabinet-sized drawer.

What stood out about Bob was his sedate, unflappable, becalmed, almost comatose demeanor. This intrigued me since I had just arrived from the guts-and-glory of the Army Airborne Infantry.

Over a period of months, I observed Bob come in at 8:30 a.m. and leave at 5:00 p.m. sharp. He never confronted anyone on any issue. He was unfailingly polite, warm and courteous. He did exactly what he was told to do, no more and no less. When I asked him why he wasn't excited about the latest project we were working on, he replied with a warm smile, indicating that I should go at it and he would watch from the sidelines.

It finally hit me. Bob was waiting for retirement. He didn't enjoy his job or dislike his job. He was basically collecting a paycheck and waiting until it was over—this whole "work for pay" thing.

Bob's whole approach shocked me. When I asked what motivated him, he perked up and mentioned his two grandchildren and how, in a little over three years, he would retire and spend more time with them and his wife. Work was just a waiting game for him.

Bob was one of the influences on my seeking self-employment after only one year in the corporate world. I'm not saying there is no satisfaction in a large public company, only that Bob's mode of operation appeared so abysmal and self-destructive to me.

Bob was following a well-worn path trod by others. He did what he was told to do and waited for the next project or assignment. He took on only minimal responsibility and reacted to every situation. He was an Indian— not a Chief.

There are many Bobs out there today. Compounding the problem, most are more than three years away from retirement and many of them are unhappy.

The Conference Board reported on February 8, 2005, that only half of all Americans are satisfied with their jobs, down from nearly 60% in 1995. "Rapid technological changes, rising productivity demands, and changing employee expectations have all contributed to the decline in job satisfaction," said Lynn France, director of the Conference Board's Consumer Research Center. Much of this unhappiness is the direct result of a lifetime spent acting as an Indian and not as a Chief.

Chiefs are leaders. Indians are followers. Chiefs are proactive. Indians are reactive. Chiefs take on full responsibility. Indians limit or avoid responsibility. Chiefs strive to create value and expand their growth. Indians keep their noses clean and maintain the status quo.

I could go on, but you get the point.

To help understand how to be a Chief in the work place, first we need to understand the work place of the 21st century.

In Malcolm Gladwell's 2000 book, *The Tipping Point*, he writes about Dunbar's Number. Robin Dunbar, a British anthropologist, determined that the cognitive limit of individuals with whom one person can maintain a stable relationship is approximately 150 people. What is interesting about this number is that it is approximately the average size of ancient hunter-gatherer groups and tribes. It's also the basic unit size of the professional armies in Roman antiquity and the basic company size in the U.S. Army and Marine Corps.

Why is this so important? It is important because in a workplace with 1,500 employees, you and I can only effectively have relationships with 150 of them. The rest are, in effect, strangers. Gladwell mentions, as an example, Microsoft's years of buying out many small companies. Instead of incorporating them into Microsoft, these companies continued to operate as close-knit groups. Likewise, other large companies often seek to divide their departments into organizations no larger than 200 individuals, to retain this air of collegiality and closeness—thereby cultivating environments conducive for Chiefs.

We can learn to be Chiefs by recognizing our own strengths. There are two diagnostic tools available today to help us determine our striving instincts.

One is the Kolbe A Index cognitive evaluation, which can be taken online at Kolbe.com in about 20 minutes. For over a decade, we have used Kolbe with clients, as well as new hires, with very good results. Basically, the Kolbe profile provides an analysis of our natural way of operating if left to our own devices. Usually, each of us initiates behavior in one of four quadrants: As a fact finder, a follow-through, a quick start, or an implementer. Many companies use these profiles to match employees with positions within the company. We tend to perform better, are happier, and experience less stress when we are allowed to do what comes naturally. When hiring, the key is to not focus totally on what the résumé records as employment history, but rather on how individuals are "hard-wired" to operate as Chiefs, not just fill positions for a bigger pay check.

The second diagnostic tool we use, called Strengths

Finder, is offered by the Gallup Organization. You can learn more about the research behind it in the book *Strengths Finder 2.0* (2007) by Tom Rath. This profile may be completed online in about 45 minutes. Research has identified 34 different strengths. Upon completing the online profile, one's top five strengths are identified in numbered order. The results are uncanny and very useful. Using them, one can convert a hierarchical organizational chart into an entrepreneurial flat structure, identifying the Chief strengths of each worker.

The great companies of today are all becoming de-centralized and customized, pushing responsibility down to the rank and file. Blame it on the microchip. In past years, companies used few Chiefs and many Indians. Today we need to have more Chiefs than Indians. Indian-style jobs are being exported overseas or being eliminated by new technology. The non-Chiefs literally have a price on their heads, and that price is measured globally each day. When that price is lower somewhere else, including shipping and delivery, it is just a matter of time before jobs are eliminated.

At one time there was a program on the Travel Channel, "Made in America," with host John Ratzenberger. John, you may recall, played Cliff Clavin, the postman in the 1980s sitcom "Cheers." Each week on "Made in America," John highlighted a few American companies that manufacture products made here in the United States. Now, I can say I was skeptical about the program at first, with all the negative statistics about the decline of the U. S. manufacturing sector over the past 30 years (from 40% of American jobs in 1970 to 17% today).

First, John met with the staff at Lyon & Healy Harps, which makes musical harps here in Chicago. The company's process is amazing—from drying specialty spruce wood for a year, to hand-sculpting it into intricate designs, followed by a specialized assembly of the thousands of instrument moving parts into a truly unique finished product. A 10-year apprentice program is required before anyone can become a master sculptor. The individual specialized jobs within the assembly process (where it takes six months to produce a harp) require extensive training. Each person in each position acts as a Chief, custom-working each unique job, all by hand. The harps are sold to symphony orchestras throughout the world. These jobs will not be outsourced to China or India. There simply is too much Chief functionality required to produce such a fine, delicate, melodious instrument.

John also featured a Red Wing Shoes factory and a Wilson Sporting Goods manufacturing plant that makes NFL footballs. Both Red Wing and Wilson buy specialty rawhide and leather accessories that are hand-cut and crafted into boots and footballs. What was interesting about each company was the size of the staff (Dunbar's Number 150) and the high number of Chief positions.

The final piece of the Chief puzzle is education—that is, continuing education, not just any education. Going out and obtaining an MBA, just because there is a pay increase, is okay; but that may only be a start. Adult education is one of the fastest-growing industries in the United States, and for good reason; it is a *requirement* in today's global economy.

If you are a 45-year-old "Bob," you will be out of a job before age 50. No one can just show up for a pay check any longer. The 21st century worker has to be a Chief. Chiefs are constantly upgrading their skills.

In 1986 I kept track of my clients and prospective new clients in a custom-made shoe box with yellow index cards, known as "The One Card System." This was the best client relationship management (CRM) system available 20 years ago. Today I have two flat-panel 19-

inch screens with a multifunctional CRM program, high-speed Internet access, an e-mail/calendar, and a comprehensive electronic filing program and Mind Map display program.

These tools allow our office staff to perform tasks efficiently and communicate effectively with our clients, service providers and partners.

We all need to be Chiefs. Indians don't last long with us or in many other firms.

It is imperative for 21st-century workers to continue to educate themselves by reading books, listening to CDs, signing up for informal/formal education, and seeking out and receiving regular mentoring, at least monthly.

Keep an open mind. Listen carefully and learn rapidly. Plan positively and take appropriate action.

Carpe diem. Seize the day!

Are You Lucky?

Life is fraught with dangers.

Although we attempt to avoid disappointments, failures and severe personal challenges, they occur anyway.

Frankly, we are not in control of much that happens in our daily lives. We seek to control our mental state, some of our routines such as sleeping, exercising and eating, but most everything else lies just outside of our full control.

We are on a long voyage that at times is calm, breezy or stormy, with many adventures and misadventures. The real key is how we address each of these challenges. How do we cope, then pick ourselves back up and continue the journey?

To this point, we have covered the life cycles that

accompany our learning and earning years. This next section primarily deals with the art of risk management. As we journey through life, how do we address risks as they occur and how do we avoid becoming victims of circumstances beyond our control?

This is the time to be honest with ourselves. When negative events occur, we first acknowledge, and then accept the state we are in, and finally look to the future for solutions that will keep us on our chosen path.

Let's begin with luck.

Luck is a word commonly used to describe unusually good fortune that seemingly happens by chance. The definition of *luck* in Webster's dictionary is "to prosper or succeed especially through chance or good fortune" and "to meet with or produce unforeseen success."

I submit—luck is not winning the lottery. It is not landing the dream job. It is not buying the next Microsoft stock at the IPO (initial public offering) and holding it to see the investment grow by 40,000%. It is not catching a "break."

On August 18, 2004, Paul Hamm was in first place after the first three apparatuses in the men's gymnastics all-around competition during the Summer Olympics in Athens. Then disaster struck on the vault. Paul did not "stick" his landing. Not only that—he actually fell backwards into one of the judges, who for a moment put his hands out to stop him from rolling off the mat into his judge's chair. Paul did his obligatory final stand with arms outstretched and waited for his score. The score came in low—so low that Paul went from first place to 12th place in the standings after four events.

The announcers quickly began to lament that Paul's quest for a gold medal was unequivocally over. Maybe—just maybe—he had a very slim chance to win the bronze medal. His brother, Morgan, watching in the stands along with other American attendees and those viewing at home, released a collective sigh.

Tough story. How "unlucky." Now our hopes are on the other American to win a medal.

Paul Hamm, however, was not done. In the next event, the pummel horse, Paul turned in one of the highest scores, moving into fourth place. Going into the sixth and final event, the high bar, the TV announcers reminded viewers that although mathematically it was possible for Paul to win gold, it was most certainly not probable.

Hamm then performed an almost perfect high bar routine, sticking the landing. This performance secured the gold by the tiniest of margins.

Did you exclaim: "What a lucky guy!" or "Was that a piece of luck, or what?" or "Man, was that guy lucky!" No doubt there were some watching who did.

After the competition, Paul was questioned about his thoughts after the vault fall, as well as a judge's error. He said that he had learned to never give up, that a lot could happen before all was said and done. He was also surprised, genuinely surprised, to learn he had won the gold. Paul had completely locked his mind onto performing each exercise to the best of his ability. He lost track of the scores.

He was not lucky. Paul had a plan to win gold. He focused on that plan, maintained his poise and motivation, and the resulting "luck" appeared magically. Paul created his "luck." A classic Olympic moment.

Twenty-four years earlier, in Lake Placid, New York, at the 1980 Winter Olympics, a young underdog United States hockey team, comprising college hockey players, won the gold medal by beating the powerhouse Soviet

Union. This was before there were professional athletes competing on dream teams. The movie, "Miracle," released in 2004, starring Kurt Russell as the Olympic coach, showed the ruthless determination and crippling practices endured daily by these young men for the six months prior to the Olympic Games. Each Olympic hockey game was a nail-biter. Each time, the United States came from behind in the third period to win against supposedly superior teams. Was the success the result of luck? Or careful preparation, total commitment and sheer determination?

During the late '90s, many investors went a little crazy during the dot-com bubble. Careful evaluation and sanity went out the door, replaced by giddiness, greed, once-in-a-lifetime opportunism and the like. In mid-1999, about a year before the stock market's peak, a man was referred to me to help him with his retirement planning. He'd just turned 61 and was planning on retiring at 62. He had $1.6 million in stock mutual funds in his 401(k) and personal investments. He had very little in cash and no bonds or bond-type investments. His plan was to retire when his stock portfolio reached $2 million. He believed, based on current market conditions, that his account would be worth $2 million in one year, since he felt almost certain he'd gain another 25% over the next 12 months. He not only wanted to keep all his assets in stock, but he also wanted to keep all his assets in stock after he retired, even though he would be drawing down $120,000 annually (8% of the value of the future $2 million portfolio).

I spent that first meeting attempting to provide him with facts, figures, historical market specifics and other tenets of investing—to no avail. He insisted we manage his portfolio 100% in stock and, particularly, in growth and dot-com stocks. During the prior five years, he had become an "expert" investor. Schooled in the new reality that all his stocks continually went up, through little effort or study of his own, he concentrated now on "Buy! Buy!! Buy!!!" online.

Our firm could not agree to be a party to the pending destruction of his asset base and bowed out of working with him. If he did find someone to help implement his plan, it is likely his retirement vision has changed drastically. Alas, this gentleman could have created "luck" by making prudent decisions to rebalance his portfolio.

In one of his noon radio broadcasts, Paul Harvey once told the "rest of the story" about a man whose luck turned from bad to good through wise actions. At the end of the segment, he offered his own definition of luck as "when chance meets opportunity."

Try for a moment to replace the word *luck* with *opportunity* in your vocabulary. There are many lucky circumstances that suddenly present themselves to those prepared to take advantage of them. Is winning the lottery luck? No, it's a random activity not dissimilar to being struck by lightning. So how does real luck work? How does one take advantage when chance meets opportunity? What is the essence behind these tenets of luck? The answer: Controlling your thoughts and actions.

We create our own luck. Great results, however, do not come solely from hard work and honest, sincere dealings. These elements also require a definitive plan: A controlled thought process seeking out a defined result that will be pursued regardless of the negative "noise" from friends, relatives, the media and life experiences. It takes persistence, coupled with positive thought and pinpoint focus on the end result.

On September 28, 1928, Alexander Fleming awoke just after dawn as he normally did and set off for his laboratory to continue investigating the properties of

Staphylococci bacteria. Fleming, a professor of bacteriology at St. Mary's Hospital in London, was conducting experiments to determine how to kill bacteria within the human body, such as the common staph infection.

Having just returned from an extended vacation, Fleming entered his lab and found many of his culture dishes contaminated with a fungus. He threw the dishes into a disinfectant, which he later retrieved to show a visitor who stopped off to look at his current experiment.

Fleming then noticed a zone around the fungus where the bacteria did not seem to grow. He proceeded to isolate an extract from the mold, correctly identifying it as being from the *Penicillium* genus.

Thus was born penicillin, the first antibiotic that later went into mass production during World War II, saving countless men from infections resulting from battlefield injuries.

What does this story share in common with luck? Fleming's struggle to find a solution to bacterial infections combined *uncertainty, preparedness* and *opportunity*.

Fleming faced uncertainty, but was prepared. The opportunity presented itself and he took decisive action.

He grasped how these three elements interact to produce positive results.

We have read how other renowned people—Henry Ford, Jonas Salk, Barbara McClintock, Bill Gates, Abraham Lincoln and many other Americans—during times of uncertainty, pressed forward prepared to meet opportunities. —Whether it was bringing automobiles to the masses, finding a polio vaccine, explaining genetic recombination, installing a computer in every home, or freeing oppressed slaves.

Each person struggles with uncertainty.

As we all know, history repeats itself, but never precisely in the same way. For nearly two years, we have been reminded daily of the unprecedented times in which we now live. Today is "history in the making." This is not dissimilar to previous experiences such as the Internet revolution and ensuing tech bubble, the fall of communism and resulting new world order, the stagflation of the '70s, the Vietnam War, World War II and the preceding Great Depression, and World War I before that. I could keep going—you get the picture. —New time, new place, human suffering, human achievement, uncertainty, fear and trepidation.

Changing the Conversation

So what are we so worried about? Haven't we been here many, many times before?

Now, I am going to write something that may initially shock you, but here goes....The world is becoming more and more uncertain. That is correct—we live in a world today that would make our great-grandparents yearn for the Dark Ages. Everything moves and changes at a faster rate.

In 1965, Gordon Moore established his now famous Moore's Law, which states that an integrated circuit's computer processing capacity doubles every two years. Today, 45 years later, even he might be astounded that it still holds true. If Moore's Law were a stock purchased for $100 in 1965, it would now be worth approximately $600 million. That is how incredible the change we are now experiencing is impacting our world today. As the saying goes, "Success favors the prepared mind." Another old adage, "Change is the only constant in life."

Luck is created. It comes through persistent effort, dogged determination, reasonable thought, and generous giving—sometimes at one's peril.

In June 1999, my nephew Mike joined the U.S. Army and

became part of the prestigious 82nd Airborne Division at Fort Bragg. In 2002, his unit was sent to Afghanistan to help in the mop-up of Taliban fighters hiding out in the mountainous areas near the Pakistan border.

In November 2002, Mike's squad was on a routine mission of a house search for Taliban living among the villagers. Two Afghan soldiers knocked on the door of one particular house, the door opened, and they were immediately killed by small arms fire. Mike's entire squad instantly came under attack from small arms fire and grenades. His team leader was seriously wounded by a grenade and needed help fast. Mike ran to his aid and was able to remove him from the line of fire, with the help of other squad members, to an awaiting medevac helicopter. But just as Mike arrived by his side and began to protect his team leader, another grenade exploded, wounding Mike. He sustained minor injuries from grenade shrapnel.

His quick action and immediate response was the reason his team leader is alive today, rather than being counted as another statistic in the War on Terror. Mike volunteered for his military duties, and it was this same giving that saved his team leader's life. He created an opportunity to save a life while possibly forfeiting his own. His team leader received "luck" that day in Afghanistan, delivered by someone who understood the law of giving.

Giving is one of those keys to creating luck. To give is to provide aid to others. In providing that, many new doors are opened. Goal-focused individuals always create a future that's bigger than their past. They are perceptive individuals who have bent their will and their being to make a better future.

As Americans cope with the world's recent economic tailspin, we may at times feel frustrated, but as New York Times journalist Thomas Friedman wrote recently in his "Paging Uncle Sam" column, "at no time in the last 50 years has the world ever seen us as more important." He quotes a senior South Korean official: "The U.S. is still No. 1 in military, No. 1 in economy, No. 1 in promoting human rights, and No. 1 in idealism. Only the U.S. can lead the world. No other country can. China can't. The E.U. is too divided, and Europe is militarily far behind the U.S. So it is only the United States….We have never had a more unipolar world than we have today."

Friedman goes on to quote Lee Hong-koo, South Korea's former ambassador to Washington: "There is no one who can replace America. Without American leadership, there is no leadership. That puts a tremendous burden on the American people to do something positive...."

By our preparedness and willingness to pick up this gauntlet in uncertain times, we can create exciting new opportunities for growth.

We can create good luck for ourselves and others.

Buying into America

A question frequently asked by my clients is, "Should I continue to invest in stock markets?"

The real question is, "Is it okay to continue investing in assets that can decline in value or do nothing for long periods of time?"

This uncertainty, of course, is most often expressed during periods of heightened risk (i.e., after Black Monday in 1987, the invasion of Kuwait in 1991, the tech bubble implosion in 2000, and the credit crisis of 2008). There's always some piece of negative news that can cause concern, even when markets are trending upwards.

So why do we continue to stay the course? Let's take a look at why buying into America is a risk we must consider taking.

When I began my last year at West Point, I was assigned to the cadet regimental staff as the recreation services officer, otherwise known as "lieutenant fun" (they had me pegged early on!). As the school year began, we met with the Executive Regimental Tactical Officer, Major Crocker. To a bunch of hard-charging 21 year olds, this blood-and-guts major was a tough character. I'll never forget how he opened the first meeting. He simply said, "You are now *them!*"

We sat there in silence not understanding the meaning of those words. He went on to explain that we were no longer the rank and file "us." As West Point seniors, we had arrived and were now "them." I remember not liking the tone of this declaration. I didn't want to be "them." I liked being "us." The "us" had no responsibility. The "us" could complain about "them." The bar was now raised— *we* had to set the standard. We were the leaders, the guys who were responsible for our unit's performance. We were now the "bad guys," the people who made the "us" do unpleasant tasks.

The United States is often the "them" on the world stage, whether we like it or not. The rest of the world watches, admires, emulates and, of course, resents us.

There is no escaping being "them." Either one embraces it or steps aside.

There are many among us who have embraced the role of setting the standard and have realized much success in our personal and business endeavors. By and large, the United States comprises individuals who epitomize the ideals of freedom, hard work, separation of church and state, and climbing to the top through hard work. There have been repeated generations of immigrants who have traveled to the United States and settled here for these same reasons.

Understanding and buying into America was engrained into me at a very early age. As I mentioned before, the memory of watching the Mercury, Gemini and, finally, the Apollo space programs put a man on the moon still fills me with a sense of excitement and "Wow!" Today, I continue to feel humbled by the educational opportunities afforded me through high school, followed by a four-year West Point education. Opportunities in this country are limitless. If we look around us, we continue to see the positive energy generated by many of our young people as well as our newest citizens who have reached our shores.

When I turned 16 in the spring of 1973, I was immersed in the traditional search for a summertime job. My aunt worked in a Greek bakery, keeping the books for the owner and his family. She was able to help secure a part-time job for me sweeping and cleaning up after the long day's shift. By the time summer vacation arrived, I actually started to work full-time rolling and pressing large vats of bread dough, loading and unloading the oven, and packing breads and rolls into bags for delivery the following morning.

What an exposure to the world of work! There were a dozen employees. On the day shift that began at 3:30 a.m. and ended at 6 p.m., I was the only employee who hadn't emigrated to this country. There were Greek, Polish, Italian and Cuban immigrants. These people worked very hard. Their average hourly pay as non-owners was between $1.75 and $2.00. The first 40 hours of each week was paid at regular wages. Overtime was figured at time-and-a-half and double on Saturday and Sunday. The average employee worked between 60 and 70 hours per week. Working conditions were difficult at best: A lot of physical labor, lifting 100-lb. bags of flour, working in front of an oven at an average temperature of 110 degrees F. Bathroom breaks were the only breaks allowed. Meals took 15 minutes or less in the vicinity of one's work station, since there was no lunch room. The memory of watching the Greek immigrant baker work up to 80 hours per week to support his wife and two small children continues to have a profound effect on me even today.

Despite these long hours in cramped and hot conditions, everyone was happy! Yes, everyone felt fortunate to be able to support themselves and their families. In the process, I gained a true understanding and new appreciation for the legions of immigrants before me who had built this country into what we experience today.

After I left the military in the mid '80s and began my career in the business world, my wife and I lived in Chicago's northwest suburbs. Weekly over a six-year period, I dropped off my shirts at a modest strip mall dry-cleaning business owned by a Korean immigrant. Eventually, my wife and I moved closer to my office in the more affluent northern suburbs. When I mentioned to the owner that I'd need to shift my business elsewhere, he surprised me. He and his family were moving to the northern suburbs as well. The American Dream was hard at work.

This industrious dry-cleaning owner wanted the best for his 14-year-old son. It was now July. The family was closing on its new home in August, just in time to enroll their son in the freshman class of one of the Midwest's top high school districts. The parents well understood the value of a first-class education, to further The Dream. Instinctively, they credited the sacrifices of America's Revolutionary and Civil Wars, and the trials and perils of the conflicts and hard times that had followed. They wanted their son to know this legacy also, to value it, and build upon it.

—To buy into America.

The United States has one of the world's highest immigration rates. In the 1970s, there was talk of declining population in our country as well as in Europe, due to projected lower birth rates. The figure that indicates a nation at parity (neither growth nor decline) is a 2.2 replacement rate. In 1997, the U.S. had a replacement rate of 2.3, and Europe, 1.6. Currently, both numbers remain virtually the same. What the numbers show is that the above-average rate of births for first-generation immigrants in the United States is offsetting the lower birth rate of established American families.

Changing the Conversation

Economists believe immigration is good because it maintains the supply of labor. Is it really good, though? Recent comments by politicians and news media columnists seem to be trying to stir up a controversy to the contrary.

A growing pool of human capital is vital. At America's current rate of increase, there are and will be more workers generating economic output tomorrow, fueled by the larger families of first-generation immigrants.

Foreigners who are not emigrating to the United States are sometimes sending their children to American universities. As noted previously, the secondary school system in America (grades 7-12) ranks only 18th in the world. The rhetoric concerning this apparent deficiency ebbs and flows between elections. Meanwhile, private school enrollment and home-schooling have been on the rise for the past decade.

Nicholas Negroponte, creator of MIT Media Lab, points out that the more culturally harmonious and homogeneous a nation becomes, the less innovation takes place. So, by that yardstick, a diversity of academically challenging teaching experiences accelerates thinking and creativity.

The United States is still the best-educated country in the world, not by brilliant academic standards, but due to its large number of educated, knowledgeable workers. China has 1.5 million college students in a nation of 1.3 billion people. America has 12 million college students in a population of 300 million. We are not the best educated, but as Negroponte points out, one-third of all Nobel Prizes have been awarded to Americans. Ambition and a strong work ethic are still defining characteristics of Americans (not just recent immigrants).

Today, Americans work on average 250 more hours annually than they worked in 1972. While the rest of the developed world is slowing down, Americans continue to push forward.

One major impediment today to the "buy into America" theme is—most unfortunately—the growing entitlement mindset. Are today's children too removed from prior generations' sacrifice and hard work? A friend of mine recently recounted a visit she had with a relative, who was complaining about being one-upped by newer, immigrant employees at the manufacturing firm where she works. Her angst was caused by these workers not taking the breaks they were "supposed" to take. From her viewpoint, the new workers must take their breaks because they were making those who took breaks "look bad." How dare they violate this unwritten "rule"!

Again, a reminder: As a nation, we must continue to strive, grow and innovate or we will fade away into perilous decline, as has happened with many developed countries.

"Buying into America" is to buy into all that America represents. In an earlier chapter, I cited Indian-born writer and thinker Dinesh D'Souza and his fine book, *What's So Great About America*. D'Souza arrived in the United States at age 18 as a foreign exchange student and never left. He embraced all that America is about, both the good and the bad. In India, his native land, he would still be living within the same two square kilometers where he was born, in an arranged marriage. Instead, he is a brilliant essayist who epitomizes the characteristics of youth, diversity and innovative collaboration.

Now—to answer that question about what should be done with our investments today. The answer is: It depends.

If you believe in buying into America, then over time your investments (if structured prudently) will pan out and your risk will be rewarded. If you don't buy into

America, then search for another economy and way of life and buy into it.

The defining characteristics of our country continue to be a strong work ethic, dedication, devotion to duty, perpetual innovation, energy, optimism and an unshakable drive to constantly search for a better way of life.

What other country offers such high prospects for product innovation, expanding economic output, rising standard of living, and the corresponding appreciation of equity investments in business, real estate and other assets in a timely repayment, with interest, of funds borrowed to fuel these enterprises?

Greater perspective on how to think about one's investments and one's life, as they relate to mitigating risk and curbing complexity, follows in the next chapter.

Understanding Complexity—And Taming It

Complexity is the bane of our daily life.

So many decisions, so much confusing input, so little time.

And our world—already complex before the microchip's invention—now runs on computer steroids.

Moreover, processing power doubles every second year (Moore's Law). New computer technology is drastically altering our lives. Social networking sites, video games, e-mail, cell phones and the like have utterly changed our social structures.

When I watch 20-somethings in a restaurant—two on their cell phones, one texting and one Twittering—I wonder if they are even sharing a meal together.

Change seems easier for the younger generation. They have never known what it is like not to be totally connected 24-7.

This makes me harken back to an era when we actually poked fun at the ridiculousness of complexity.

Rube Goldberg was a popular American cartoonist, engineer, inventor and author who received a 1948 Pulitzer Prize for his political cartooning. Mr. Goldberg is best known for his cartoons depicting complex devices, which ultimately perform very simple tasks. One example of Rube Goldberg's machines was the "Self-Operating Napkin" used by Professor Butts. The "Self-Operating Napkin" activates when a soup spoon is lifted, connected to a string that is pulled, connected to a ladle that sends a biscuit flying, etc....that finally is connected to another string, which when cut, allows a pendulum with the attached napkin to swing back and forth, wiping Professor Butts' chin.

Fast forward to 2008 when we discovered how sub-prime loans were issued by banks, bought by Wall Street, repackaged into traunches that were then leveraged and sold as collateralized debt obligations and then "hedged" using further leverage and credit default swaps, with all of the above ultimately blowing up because no one really understood the financial contraption. And that is just one financial instrument!

Let's acknowledge it: Those who can meaningfully simplify our complex lives deserve laurels and applause.

Simplicity is about caring about each other enough to deliver a product or service we need or desire but that does not complicate our lives.

That is much easier said than done.

A way to simplify the lives of others may be accomplished by following the Golden Rule, "Do to others what you would like to be done to you." To understand how this actually works—this interaction and empathy for others—let us step back for a moment and look at how we are wired. As the diagram on the next page illustrates, there are three parts to our brain: the neo-cortex, the brain stem and the limbic system. The neo-cortex is our analytical "thinking" brain, the brain stem our automatic "doing" brain, and the limbic system our "emotional" brain.

So you may be asking yourself, "What does this have to do with making my life simple?" In answer to this, let us take a look at the U.S. transportation industry.

On the one hand, there are the Big Three in southeastern Michigan, and on the other there's Harley-Davidson, the motorcycle manufacturer, in southeastern Wisconsin. Over the past three decades, the Big Three have been declining steadily while at the same time Harley-Davidson continues to grow

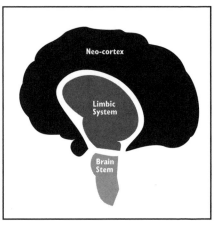

steadily. Four Midwest manufacturing companies: All providing transportation and producing vehicles in the United States—yet three are struggling while the other is growing. Why is this happening?

As many of you may know, one perk of working for a U.S. automobile manufacturer is discount prices available to extended family members for the purchase of an automobile. Due to the large automobile workforce in southeastern Michigan, there are proportionally many more American-made models on the roads in the Detroit area than in other U.S. cities. So much so that it is hard to spot a Toyota Camry, the No. 1 selling car in America, in this Michigan region. The Big Three have discouraged their work force from experiencing the visceral enjoyment and thrill of a foreign car. Now, I'm not saying foreign cars are better—only that the bubble Detroit has built around its populace disconnects consumers from other offerings and their obtainable features.

On the other side of Lake Michigan, Harley-Davidson has become deeply involved with the Harley Owner's Group (HOG), listening to its suggestions about how to improve the product, providing a better offering than other leading motorcycle manufacturers. It encourages its employees to belong to local groups, and hires motorcycle enthusiasts for key positions on its staff. It understands what the motorcycle enthusiast wants, and stays in close touch with new offerings and improvements.

The difference between Detroit and Milwaukee is listening—connecting the thinking and doing brain with the emotional brain—creating an organization closely attuned to its customers by offering empathetic products and services.

Achieving simplicity is not as simple as it sounds. Just ask a frightened young couple with a sick child, dealing with tentative diagnoses, crowded hospital waiting rooms and months of complex insurance claims.

Just ask the team of doctors, seeking the optimal medical solution within the human body's complex structures of organs, tissues, cells, organelles, polymers, monomers and atoms.

Complexity—from the Latin word *complexus* meaning entwined, twisted together—always exists between order and disorder, frequently on the brink of chaos. It has to be understood and tamed.

Just think what the CT scanner's clarity has done for medical science, and the Hubble telescope's clarity for deciphering deep space.

Just think what identifying the complex ratio value of a circle's circumference to its diameter (*pi*, or approximately 3.14159) did for mathematics, science and engineering, by providing a simple numerical and physical constant.

Just think what even 3M Company's simple Post-It® Notes back in 1980 did for helping businesses and individuals easily organize and "bookmark" their daily activities.

Bain & Company, a complexity management consultant,

has found in its research of 110 companies in 17 industries ranging from cosmetics to aerospace and medical equipment to mutual funds that companies with the lowest complexity grew 30-50%, faster than their average competitors. The reason why? Too much variety (high complexity) often suggests a bigger problem: "Poor understanding of customers. By providing the right level of product variety, companies can increase sales and market share, while cutting costs."

Our complex lives, due primarily to the explosion of technological advances (I'm still resisting registering on Facebook), can be simplified if organizations continue to care about their customers. We are social beings meant to care, to think and to do. Much of the complexity we experience is due to the "take it or leave it" mentality of big business. Organizations that focus only on the bottom line do not last.

Dev Patnaik, in his recent book *Wired to Care* (2009), had this to say on our current state of corporate affairs:

> *"...most companies are corporate iguanas. It's as if they've skipped right over the limbic system to grow a neo-cortex. Corporations are ethically neutral beasts, focused on self-preservation. They're not immoral—they're amoral. They lack any sense for the impact that their actions have on others. And that goes back to how*

they're structured. They have a reptilian brain to act. They have a neocortex to think. They just don't have any way to feel. Without a limbic system, companies lack any sense of empathy or courage. They're either all neocortex, analyzing thoughtfully without the motivation to act, or reptilian, caught in a cycle of fight-or-flight responses. That's deeply unfortunate, because companies are made up of people, not iguanas. And people, not iguanas, buy products and services." (p. 115)

Enough said.

Green Bay Packers coach Vince Lombardi understood simplicity. Once he was invited to attend an NFL Coaches Conference. The event featured the coaches sharing their various strategies and techniques that made their teams successful. Eventually it was Coach Lombardi's turn. Like every other coach, he was asked, "Coach Lombardi, what strategies do you use to successfully move the football down the field when on offense?" Vince Lombardi's response: Knocking the opponent down to advance the football down the field. When asked about defense, he said his team knocks the opponent down so the football cannot be advanced down the field. Coach Lombardi was expert at simplifying the game of football. Concentrate on the basics of blocking and tackling.

Steve Jobs and Apple single-handedly dropped the music recording industry to its knees. Jobs reasoned that we don't want to listen to all the songs recorded on the CD, just the one or two we like....And iTunes was born. Hear a song you like. Immediately download it for a small fee and enjoy!

The French wine industry is renowned for its centuries-long tradition of offering more than 700 different varieties of wines by geographic location, type of grape and vintage. Only the very well-educated wine connoisseur is able to select and enjoy the right wine. A little company in Australia, Yellow Tail, reasoned that most of us just want a good riesling, chardonnay or merlot. Over the past five years, Yellow Tail has captured a sizable part of French wine industry sales by simplifying the offerings for anyone to understand and enjoy. Simplicity—not complexity.

Any company or industry that still clings to timeworn complex models of doing business has its days numbered. Consumers embrace organizations that simplify our complex lives and make it easy for us to understand, make a decision, and enjoy the outcome.

—A viable mandate for all of us going forward.

Focus on the simple. Delegate the complex. Relax and enjoy. Then repeat.

One fond and final recollection—recalling Winston Churchill. Of course, during wartime, complexity can spell defeat. Churchill told his aides he had no time to read their ponderous reports. He demanded war plans on single sheets of paper.

On October 29, 1941, he agreed to speak at Britain's elite Harrow School. It was after the London Blitz. The core message of his brief speech:

> *"Never give in. Never give in. Never, never, never, never—in nothing, great or small, large or petty—never give in, except to convictions of honour and good sense. Never yield to force. Never yield to the apparently overwhelming might of the enemy."*

He soon sat down.

Silence.

Suddenly, thunderous applause erupted for his remarks.

Churchill knew what really mattered.

As British Prime Minister in the midst of a world war's complex strife and anxiety-ridden confusion, his solution was defiant.

And simple.

Navigating Storms and Currents

On April 11, 1970, Apollo XIII blasted into space with astronauts Jim Lovell, John Swigert and Fred Haise aboard. Launches at the Kennedy Space Center had been watched by millions of Americans over the previous decade as part of the Mercury, Gemini and Apollo space programs. As a nation, we had fulfilled President Kennedy's dream of sending men to the moon and returning them safely to Earth within the decade.

It was the "returning safely to Earth" part that looked in perilous jeopardy when disaster struck on April 13th.

The ship's oxygen tanks had exploded into space, leaving the crew with only three hours of oxygen to return to Earth. The support team at Houston's Mission Control sprang into action. They had to figure out how to maneuver the ship around the moon, then proceed on a return trajectory to Earth, literally with both arms tied behind their backs. Lovell and his crew were forced into the Lunar Module to conserve their oxygen. They had to resort to primitive celestial navigation techniques.

I remember the newspaper headlines and accompanying articles stating that one minor miscalculation could mean missing the Earth by thousands of miles, to forever float into space.

These were scary headlines. It was one of the worst events we witnessed as Americans prior to September 11, 2001. Then came the Director of Flight Operations Gene Kranz's famous line: "Failure is not an option."

He rallied the Houston support team to come up with solution after solution after solution to handle all of the problems jeopardizing the crew's safe return. As a result of the quick thinking and calm resolve of three astronauts and thousands of support personnel, Apollo XIII landed safely in the Pacific Ocean April 17, 1970. The mission was deemed a successful failure. The success part was entirely related to how all these people, individually and as a group, handled the bad news.

When confronted with bad news, many of us feel a physical change take over our bodies. An emotional "down" takes place, stress builds, blood pressure increases, and we feel our faces begin to flush. Some of us experience increased perspiration, a bad feeling in our stomachs and, in severe cases, become physically ill and depressed.

The interesting thing about these seemingly involuntary reactions is that they just happen as if we have no control over our bodies, thoughts or emotions.

In reality, emotional outbursts are often part of our conscious reactions. Some bad news will be with us for months or years, as in the sudden death of a loved one or the onset of a serious illness. Other bad news can be over in a matter of minutes. Much of our reaction has to do with a level of preparedness and experience in handling such disappointment.

My first professional "bad news" experience was the stock market crash of Black Monday, October 19, 1987. It seems like ancient history now, but it was very serious at the time. You may recall the Dow Jones Industrials dropping 508 points, or losing 22.6% on that day, reminiscent of the October 1929 crash that preceded the Great Depression. Within days after Black Monday, newspapers popped up spelling out impending doom, predicting the start of the second Great Depression.

Gary Klaben

On October 19, 1987, there were three things that could be clearly seen from outer space: the Great Wall of China, the Roman aqueducts, and the human line forming around Fidelity Investments in Boston. All joking aside—it was almost impossible to get through to the major no-load mutual funds using their 800 numbers. A tremendous number of investors suddenly wanted to sell their stock mutual funds and buy into money markets. Millions wanted out of stock immediately after stock reports worsened throughout that Monday.

Actually, theirs was the diametrically wrong reaction. They should have been buying stock mutual funds. By the end of the day on Black Monday, it was a rare opportunity to buy stocks at great prices. But, and this is a big *but*, investors needed to keep their cool while all those around them were panicking.

Part of our problem with these typical knee-jerk reactions is our "lizard brain." The lizard brain is that part of the brain that's at the top of the spinal column, signaling adrenaline and the fight-or-flight response. A few millennia ago, the lizard brain served as a critical survival instinct for early humans. It is this same instinct that caused the death of 21 people in a Chicago night club in 2004 when pepper spray, used to break up a fight, spurred hundreds of frightened people to try and exit the night club at the same time.

Our emotional response to stock market bad news is partly due to the intangible nature of stocks and other investments. We have a hard time with intangibles. On the other hand, real estate is tangible. By 2007, the U.S. real estate bubble had burst. Yet millions of Americans did not place "for sale" signs on their property. The major reason: Real estate is tangible. It's real. You can see it, touch it, feel it, and live in it. Just because reports showed real estate prices going down in value, this was not enough to set off a domino effect of selling. We look at our property and say, "What does it matter, still looks the same as yesterday, I am in no hurry to sell. When the real estate market bounces back, then I'll consider it."

This is not true for stocks. Stocks can't be seen. Sure, we can see and touch the products produced by companies, but the stocks can't be felt, or experienced, or used for shelter. There are investors out there who still have stock certificates they will not relinquish, primarily due to the perceived benefits of the tangibility of the paper.

What we can't see, touch, taste or feel *scares* us.

So, it doesn't take much to start a stampede of people heading off for the exits, like lemmings jumping off the cliff. People have a difficult time coming to grips with stocks, the notion of absentee ownership in a "real" business, and a share of a future stream of "real and sustainable profits." All we see are declining prices!

It is amazing what results from bad news. The Australian actor Russell Crowe played the part of boxer James Braddock in the movie "Cinderella Man." James Braddock was a contender for the heavyweight title at the start of the Great Depression. Just a few years later, with a wife and three children, he was penniless, barely scraping by in New York City. The bad news of the Depression completely engulfed him and his family.

The Cinderella part of the story took place in 1933 when he resurrected his spirit and fighting skills to box Max Baer for the heavyweight title. Max Baer was a huge powerful fighter who had previously killed two men in the boxing ring. When the press quizzed Braddock about the "why" of his attempted comeback, he did not reply, "To become a champion" or "To go out on top." His motivation: "Milk." He needed to save his family.

James Braddock went on to win the fight as a huge

underdog. He never looked back.

Bad news does not define us. How we react to bad news is what defines us.

There are generally four different types of reactions that most of us exhibit when confronted with bad news. The first, "deer in the headlights," sees us put our hands up and take cover like a wounded boxer, taking blow after blow without any retaliation. We are frozen by our fear. We sort of resemble James Braddock—before he found his resolve.

The second reaction is to play the "blame game." Someone is to blame for this travesty of justice and they are going to pay. Rather than pick up the pieces and move on, we look for scapegoats and expend emotional energy and economic resources in finger-pointing and litigation. We spend too much time asking "why" this could happen and too little time asking "How do I pick up the pieces?"

A third response is to hunker down and wait for the storm to pass. When we come out of the shelter after the storm passes, we resolve to work with what we have, and try to survive and rebuild our lives. This may be a passive response, but it is certainly more pragmatic than not fighting back at all or doing nothing but whining about it.

The last example is to view bad news as an opportunity. These are your glass-half-full individuals. They perceive opportunity when everyone else sees despair, destruction and contraction. They adapt, innovate and begin new businesses and new lives. You may not be aware that there are more entrepreneurs created during bad economic times than good times—*there are!* Losing one's job is often the positive impetus leading people to finally strike out on their own.

Most life lessons are learned as a result of bad news. We fail at something, regroup, reassess, then move on to the new. This never-ending process of elimination and new selection echoes in the sermons preached by some of our parents: "Your future choices are limited or multiplied by your past choices."

The key ingredient of success: Our reaction to bad news or failure. As Dale Carnegie liked to say, "Look at the worst case scenario and then make the best of it!"

If handed a lemon, make lemonade—or better yet, a spiced lemon smoothie.

Changing the Conversation

Along with death and taxes, setbacks and tragedy will always be constants in our lives, not something our federal government can legislate away.

Americans are an interesting lot. When serious bad news affects our citizens, we put down partisan signs and jump into action. During and after the 9/11 terrorist attacks, normally gruff, brusque New Yorkers became civil, caring and concerned neighbors for the families and businesses struck by this tragedy. Although the 2005 federal response to Hurricane Katrina, which devastated New Orleans and the lower Mississippi delta region, was slow, not so for Americans. Thousands of volunteers from charities, churches, social organizations and individuals acting on their own assisted those affected by the storm. The collective response of America was unparalleled.

As a nation, we continually display our ability to step up—to manage bad news by taking positive action.

Age of Art and Heart

I first learned about the great Renaissance poets, composers and painters in fifth grade. What incredible art these great masters had produced! Then my teacher changed subjects. My school day finished with arithmetic, English and science. Yet, at home, I found myself daydreaming about the Renaissance period. Suddenly my brain was jolted back to reality. My mother's voice, "Study your science, math and English if you want to grow up and be somebody...support a family...live in the real world."

So I dutifully finished grammar school, high school and West Point, graduating with a Bachelor of Science in General Engineering. I felt ready to tackle the Industrial Age—those exciting Renaissance masters largely pushed aside.

Now, I find the world has changed. The Renaissance is

back. We are no longer in the Industrial Age. We are still in the Information Age, but even that is fading quickly into what is now being called the Conceptual Age.

Nothing ever stays the same. Change has always been the operative word of the day. We see this reality played out in the 1967 movie, "The Graduate." Dustin Hoffman plays a depressed college graduate, Benjamin Braddock. Benjamin has a conversation with Mr. McGuire who gives him one piece of advice: "Plastics." Ah, yes, plastics, the mantra of the new Industrial Age. Benjamin had a choice. He could either get on, get out of the way, or get run over by this new train of change.

Since 1967, the train has continued to pick up speed. New homes are now almost twice the size of homes built in the 1970s. One-car garages have been replaced with three-car garages. Today we have digital phones, plasma/LCD TVs, personal computers, DSL/high-speed cable Internet access, microwave ovens, iPods, cell phones, iPads and much, much more. The Information Age has created immense opportunities and efficiencies for corporate and service industry jobs.

The Internet's introduction has created another fundamental change. It has leveled the playing field. Before the

Internet, the United States, Germany and Japan called the shots. Each country's industrial base researched, developed and created products in their respective countries. They were preferred by their citizens and shipped out to sell to the rest of the developed world. The beginning of the end of the Information Age coincided with the first decade of the Internet. Global commoditization and manufacturing of products, from sneakers to jet engines, as well as the outsourcing of such services as call centers and complex data entry, are common today.

A great example of this commoditization and globalization trend is illustrated in *The World is Flat* (2005) by Thomas Friedman. Friedman purchased a Dell notebook computer to use in writing his book. He called the Dell 800 number and spoke to a sales representative in India, named Mujteba Naqui. At the time, Dell assembled its notebook computers at six factories in Ireland, China, Brazil, the United States (two) and Malaysia. This particular order was routed to Penang, Malaysia. Dell uses multiple suppliers to ensure a constant flow of parts. Basically, the global supply chain reaches around the world and results in a notebook computer being completely assembled in the Penang factory in approximately three-to-five hours. Dell works with hundreds of other U.S. and foreign companies to deliver personal computers to homes and businesses worldwide.

Dell is an obvious success story, but what about all those middle-market companies and mom-and-pop businesses that dot the American Information Age landscape? How are they dealing with globalization? Can they compete? Are they just a bankruptcy waiting to happen, or are they the next Dell? How about the tens of millions of Americans in technical and service jobs? Are their jobs about to be outsourced or eliminated? What will they do about the future?

The answers to these questions lie in a new age, just now in its infancy. It is the Conceptual Age, or as we like to refer to it, "the age of art and heart." How do we come to grips with this new Conceptual Age? How does it affect you and me? How do we prepare ourselves to survive as employees, patrons, owners, investors, retirees, stewards and legatees in this new age?

Let's start with an examination of how we think.

From time to time, we are reminded about the two halves of our brain. When a stroke victim is paralyzed on the right side of the body, the doctor informs the family that a blood clot has damaged the left side of the brain. Physically, the right and left sides of our brain control opposite sides of our body. However, when it comes to thinking and reasoning, the left hemisphere is logical, sequential and analytical while the right hemisphere is non-linear, holistic and intuitive. We use both sides of our brain, however, to perform all tasks.

Since the dawn of the Industrial Revolution we have relied more on sequential, left-brain thinking to develop, organize and operate businesses. Our schools and universities have educated a disproportionate number of Americans in the math, engineering, science, accounting and legal fields, fostering sequential thinking. We have far fewer graduates in music and the visual performing arts.

How many parents do you know who would be enthusiastic about their child pursuing an acting career, becoming a rock star, writer or artist? Maybe we need to spend more time learning the lessons of the Renaissance than just a few weeks in the fifth grade!

In order to succeed like Dell, we must start appreciating, developing and using our intuitive right-brain capabilities. Michael Dell and company have retained their intellectual capital for design. They do not OWN the intricate process chain. Rather, they retain their knowledge and understanding of its infrastructure. This is classic right-brain, intuitive functioning. Does this mean Dell does not excel at applying sequential and analytical left-brain functions? Absolutely not. Now more than ever, it is critical to use both intuitive and sequential thinking to manage and grow a business.

Dell and other successful Conceptual Age companies have embraced the change brought about by the Internet. Others have been forced to downsize or consolidate, resulting in the elimination of jobs, especially union jobs. Since 1970, more than half of all union labor has been eliminated. This can be attributed primarily to the technological advances brought about by microprocessing.

Emotional and economic pain is experienced each day by a significant number of Americans and has sparked debate about the "fairness" of outsourcing jobs to Mexico, China, India and other countries.

First, as a nation and as a people, we must re-educate ourselves. Most new jobs are opening not in the industrial trades, but in the service industry. Obviously, we still have our work cut out for us in dealing with the social ramifications of these changes.

Change is challenging, but there is hope. We must understand that we are in a new age, a Conceptual Age, and that there are new rules. Like Benjamin from "The Graduate," we need to get on the train. It all starts with education.

Every person working in a business must create value, to ultimately remain employed. Each year, many large accounting firms electronically transfer basic income tax return work out to India because the cost is much less than using U.S. accounting labor.

Many product call centers are now located in India, Russia and Poland.

To create wealth, U.S. workers must continue to educate themselves. A degree from a four-year college or technical school is just the beginning. Job security is a function of the number of wealth-creating skill sets that one possesses. Continuous reading and taking courses in school or through the Internet is vital. Intuitive awareness and sequential skills must be improved and maintained, to avoid getting thrown off or run over by the train.

In his book, *A Whole New Mind* (2005), Daniel Pink compares two men, Paul Thompson, director of the Cooper-Hewitt Museum in New York City, and Noria

Ohga, former chairman of Sony. He examines their competitive approaches in today's global market.

Thompson comments: "Manufacturers have begun to recognize that we can't compete with the pricing, structure and labor cost of the Far East. So how can we compete? It has to be with design."

Ohga states: "At Sony, we assume that all products of our competitors have basically the same technology, price, performance and features. Design is the only thing that differentiates one product from the other in the market place."

In other words, intuitive creativity must be applied in order to win. Complete financial strategies and transactions, creative design, innovative packaging and other intellectual property are not yet being outsourced.

The computer is not able to replicate the unique functions of right-brain creativity while organizing and delivering a unique product or service.

This is the business of the future for developed nations.

When accounting firms outsource the completion of tax returns to India, the basic information is entered. The firms still retain research and decision-making skills necessary for more complicated and complex tax and accounting services.

Author Pink goes on to discuss the MFA (Master of Fine Arts) degree as the new MBA. In his opinion, there is a shortage of MFAs in the United States. Mom and Dad, maybe there is hope for your starving artist!

Robert Slee, an investment banker in Charlotte, North Carolina, provides corporate financing for middle-market, private companies. He travels America presenting all-day seminars to middle-market business owners using his mental construct, the "river of wealth." He has found that many U.S. business owners are one step away from going out of business because they are ignoring globalization. According to Slee, there are approximately 300,000 middle-market businesses in the United States, accounting for approximately 80% of new jobs each year. He is attempting to reorient these businesses and business owners from the Industrial/Information Age to the Conceptual Age.

How does one distinguish between a company such as Dell and one of these Information Age, middle-market companies? Companies that are tactical (Information

Age) will lose while those that are strategic (Dell) should win. Tactical companies that are left-brain oriented act as sergeants, perform as players, and concentrate on operations and sales. Strategic companies such as Dell are both left- and right-brain oriented, act as generals, coach the players, create fluid business models, and concentrate on marketing.

Today we live in a strategic world, yet most U.S. business owners are still acting tactically. This must change!

If you want a loan from Robert Slee to expand your business, you must be *strategic*. If you bring a Dell-type model to him, based on design and delivery, with everything else outsourced, there is a good chance he will underwrite the capital for your start-up or expansion. Financial capital is a commodity; intellectual capital is the "know how." People now get paid for their know-how.

In our society today, there's another developing trend—the quest for meaning and purpose. Our success as a country has created significant wealth. Our lifestyles are blessed with a multitude of comforts and material possessions. We have more of everything in great numbers, varieties, flavors and choices. Many of us are now asking, "What's it all about?" "What is the meaning of life?"

Ronald Inglehart, a political scientist at the University of Michigan, administers an annual world value survey. Recently, his respondents have expressed a greater concern for spiritual and non-material matters. According to one of his recent surveys, 80% of Americans think often about the meaning and purpose of life. This seems to indicate a slow shift from solely materialistic goals toward goals that also include meaning.

We find that many retirees today have become busier than they ever imagined. They spend their time with grandchildren, seeking to build relationships and pass on their knowledge and values. They volunteer at hospitals, shelters, museums and churches, not only to maintain a sense of purpose in their lives, but also to help perpetuate these institutions and what they represent. They have retired "to" something rather than "from" something.

The growth of this societal perspective offers hope in our struggle to reconcile the social and economic distortions that will continue to develop as the train rolls on.

This hope feels very real when we remember how many of us stepped up to help following Katrina in New Orleans. One man I met from Utah single-handedly saved more than 4,000 dogs in a two-week period.

Changing the Conversation

People all over the country opened their homes to displaced families. We as a people do what our government is not able to do effectively.

This is all about heart.

Understanding and harmony are expressed in music, art, entertainment and nature's grandeur. Just spend a half hour, three days in a row, watching the sun set in complete silence over mountains or the ocean. *Sheer bliss!* Travel to Rome and visit the Sistine Chapel, or the Louvre in Paris, or the Parthenon in Athens. Sail Glacier Bay in Alaska or breathe the pine-scented Appalachian air of the Great Smokies.

We as a people seem to be moving more and more each day toward greater use of our holistic and intuitive abilities.

The Renaissance is alive and well, "reappearing" in a much different form due to advances in technology.

A wondrous thing!

Retirement Yearning

Arguably the most difficult lifestyle change we experience involves moving from the "earning" stage to the "yearning" stage—otherwise known as retirement.

The latter embodies hope, belonging, desperation, anxiety, fear, freedom, joy, all tied into one package: *Retirement.*

My attention to this transition mounted following the death of my grandfather and a client.

As I grew up, my grandfather commanded a fair amount of influence on my life. He and my dad took my brother and me fishing and hunting. I sat many hours in my granddad's fishing boat listening to him and my father discuss all their adult experiences and share their views on fish lures and life.

My grandfather retired in 1965 at the age of 65 after

working 45 years for the same manufacturing company and rising to the level of foreman. He was proud of his success in providing for his family, and passed on his strong work ethic to my father and to me. Prior to retirement he was active, energetic, and fun to be around. After retirement, he slowly turned into someone I did not recognize. He spent more and more time in his air-conditioned room and his easy chair watching television, coming out only to eat and sleep. He stopped going fishing, begrudgingly went to family functions, and continued to deteriorate in mind, soul and health. He did not have Alzheimer's. He just faded away. He moved in with my parents in 1980 and died nine years later.

It still brings tears to my eyes as I think about the contrast of the years before and around retirement to particularly the last 10 years. It left a very big impression on me. I decided not to end up like my granddad.

A few years after my grandfather's death, I was referred to a new client. Prior to meeting this client, I practiced retirement planning in somewhat the same manner as other wealth advisors, concentrating on the balance sheet, cash flow, investments, taxes and all the other hard financial data.

That changed after the death of this client.

I had met with him and his wife to discuss his impending retirement, which was coming up in about 30 days. He and his spouse were very nervous about retirement, since this was such a big step. Paul had worked as a pilot flying corporate jets his entire 35-year career with the same company. At first glance, it appeared they had sufficient assets and pension to live comfortably after retiring. Our second meeting, 10 days prior to retirement, went well. Still, there was a deep-down fear being exhibited by him and his wife. We discussed his reluctance to retire. But he had committed to a specific company retirement date, and her health was not good. We set up a third meeting for two days after his retirement.

On his official retirement day, Paul left his office party, held at an airport hangar, and drove to a local convenience store for some food and provisions. At the store he parked, then immediately slumped over: A fatal heart attack. A store employee eventually noticed and alerted authorities; however, he had already died.

We have all heard stories about people dying shortly after retirement. I believe much of this has to do with facing retirement.

Changing the Conversation

Prior to the 19th century, the word *retirement* did not exist. In 1889, Chancellor Otto von Bismarck of Germany had some problems—the factories' "graybeards" of the time, after a life of back-breaking work, were slowing productivity. And, a high unemployment rate for young males saw numbers of these idle youths carouse, tear up streets and shops, and require public resources to be directed toward rebuilding. To solve these problems, Bismarck installed social security with his Old Age and Disability Insurance Law, which required older men to give up their jobs so younger men could be hired.

Before the year 1700, with high child mortality, the average life expectancy was not much past the age of 40. Of course, with advances in today's medicine, our life spans are much longer. Possibly, today's expanding work force is even growing at a rate faster than available jobs. Certainly as a result, yesteryear's nascent and novel concept of retirement is today's steadfast reality.

How does the dictionary define *retirement?* "Retire: 1) To go away, depart, for rest, seclusion or shelter; 2) To go to bed; 3) To withdraw from business or public life so as to live at leisure on one's income, savings or pension; 4) To fall back, retreat. Retired: Withdrawn; secluded."

Maybe you noticed a pattern: Go away, depart, seclusion, withdraw, fall back.

It seems like we are supposed to go away and DIE when we stop working for a living.

Forget about Chancellor Bismarck's problems. We've got a much bigger challenge here in our country. Did you know that there are approximately 38 million Americans who are 65 or older? How many of them will fit this definition of retirement? Hopefully, very few.

My grandfather's generation never believed that they would live much past age 65. It has just been in the past century that we are living longer, with those over age 100 having tripled in the past 15 years. In fact, when Social Security started in the 1930s, the government never projected Americans living more than five years on Social Security. That is why the "pay as you go" Social Security program will have to change to meet the needs of the Baby Boomers, some of whom began collecting Social Security in 2009. But that is a whole different story.

By now it may have occurred to you that maybe, just maybe, we should convince the dictionary folks to update their definitions of retirement—or at a minimum convince ourselves to change our own definitions!

A friend of mine, after attending his 40th high school reunion, related his experiences catching up with former classmates. The group was in its late 50s, so obviously many conversations touched on retirement. "Are you retiring soon?" "What is your time frame for losing that starched shirt and tie and lowering your golf handicap?"

You would never ask this question of a 75-year-old person—we all assume he or she is long retired.

My friend at his reunion, hearing the retirement question directed to him, answered: "I'm not."

He has many plans for his business over the next 25 years, into his early 80s.

His response was greeted with complete silence, a pregnant pause, then someone awkwardly changed the subject.

My friend understands. *They don't get it.* For 40 years, these classmates have been moving toward retirement, that time when one no longer has to, or is willing to, work for a paycheck. This is the next "expected" stage in life's journey. You are born, you go to school, get a job, raise a family, retire and die. Quite simple.

The "get a job" and "retire" parts both connote negatives. I, for one, find these words burdened with traditional stereotypes. I don't care for their meaning. However, this chapter will focus on retirement.

Isn't life about growth, about always moving forward? Sure, we sometimes take two steps forward then one step back. That's the definition of learning, making mistakes and gaining experience. There was that first day of kindergarten, first day of high school, first day of college, first job, marriage, having children, taking on a mortgage, watching children grow, and then grandchildren.

Each step of the way involves a challenge, new risks with new rewards, new learning and new insights.

We're hearing many of our senior clients say they have less time now than when they were working! These people have learned how to continue to grow and learn during their retirement years.

Still, there are those who believe retirement involves just an easy transition with no new challenges.

For anyone who is nearing retirement (and for those who see it in the distant future), there is something you can do right now to prepare yourself for retirement. On a recent PBS television program, teacher-author Dr. Wayne Dyer spoke about the three stages of life: The *warrior* stage, when we ask, "What's in it for me?"; the *give back* stage, "How can we help our fellow man?"; and a *spiritual* stage, "What's it all about?"

Abraham Maslow's psychological "hierarchy of needs" pyramid starts off with food and shelter, then progresses through social needs to self-actualization, and ultimately, spiritual needs.

I like to refer to these three stages as *learning, earning* and *yearning*.

Let's take a look at a practical exercise in how to think about this so-called retirement in a different way. What if retirement were viewed as a new beginning instead of simply freeing one's self from energy-draining activities? What if you were left with all the things you love and enjoy doing?

Retirement can mean retiring from all of the things you don't like doing, and continuing to do activities you love and want to do more of. Or if you prefer, freedom from those activities you don't want to do and freedom to pursue those activities you want to do more of.

It's simply about gaining more freedom.

How to get started?

Set aside a little quiet time. Give yourself 30 minutes to complete this exercise. Take out a sheet of paper and divide it into four columns. In the first column, write down "What would I immediately stop doing?" Only spend three minutes quickly writing down everything you can think of. In the second column, write down "Why would I stop doing it?" Next to each activity, write why you would stop doing that activity. Does it drain your energy because it is too complex? Do you find the activity stressful? It should take less than 15 minutes to complete these first two columns. You may end up with 10 or more activities.

In the third column, write down "What would I continue doing?"—that is, those activities you love and enjoy. Also, write down those activities you would start to pursue. Give yourself three minutes to quickly write down those activities—those you love doing and those you want to take on. In the fourth column, write down "Why would I continue or start doing?"

You should end up with four columns, many activities

that you want to stop doing, and many activities you would like to start or continue doing.

I've been working on this exercise myself for a while and have eliminated all but a few activities.

By this definition, I can imagine I'm semi-retired. However, most would consider me fully, actively working. Does this mean I am retiring? Of course not—exactly the opposite, in the traditional sense of what retirement means. When I finally eliminate all of the activities in the left-hand column, I, too, will be "retired."

This exercise, if completed properly, will clearly show what activities you need to eliminate to be "retired" or, as I like to think, "reinvented."

Until you are able to eliminate all items in column one, you have not made the transition or *reinvented yourself* for the next stage in life.

The table on page 194 illustrates the life expectancy of Boeing Aerospace retirees based on age and retirement. It is not a pretty picture. Those who retire early live proportionately longer than those who retire later. It is a sobering chart. I'm not certain if it represents conclusive evidence that life expectancy is tied to retirement age,

Age at Retirement	Average Age at Death
49.9	86
51.2	85.3
52.5	84.6
53.8	83.9
55.1	83.2
56.4	82.5
57.2	81.4
58.3	80
59.2	78.5
60.1	76.8
61	74.5
62.1	71.8
63.1	69.3
64.1	67.9
65.2	66.8

Dr. Ephrem (Siao Chung) Cheng, Actuarial Study of Age at Retirement vs. Life Span

given only Boeing Aerospace employees. However, paying heed to this cautionary chart—and seeking to eliminate activities from your own chart's left-hand column—can surely help reduce stress and increase freedom from those activities we don't want to do.

Please refer back to the chapter on goal-setting to determine how to set worthy goals and eliminate column one activities. Treat this like you do in business: Review your one-year, three-year or five-year plans in order to wipe out the first column. Go through and eliminate certain activities one by one by putting together your 90-day and 30-day action plans.

—So that, eventually, you will be in retirement mode.
—So that at the point you decide to do something different and reinvent yourself, you'll already be there!
—So that your transition can be as very smooth and enjoyable as possible.

Transitions in life are immensely difficult if we begin from a standing start.

Remember, it probably took a decade or so to gain the confidence and experience in the work place to contribute and be an effective member of an organization. It certainly took at least that long to develop survivalist parenting skills.

Time is too precious at this life-changing stage to delay or go down the wrong road.

Start this transition sooner than later by changing your own definition of retirement and by taking positive steps to pursue the things you passionately love and enjoy.

What Is Your True Worth?

Invariably, at a first meeting with a potential client, we obtain information concerning assets, income, tax returns and the like.

But jumping right into the details is not the best way to start a meaningful dialogue—though it's often the easiest way to break the ice.

A question that often hangs in the air: "What am I worth?" Well, there are many ways to answer this question. First, there is net worth, a sum of all assets minus liabilities. Most accounting professionals would agree with that definition. Then there is self worth, which of course is in the eye of the beholder.

Now, this definition is much fuzzier. It may change from time to time depending on life conditions. There are also many sub-definitions, such as emotional worth, social worth and others.

But what is your *true* worth? The answer to this question may surprise you.

My old, tattered American Heritage dictionary defines *worth* as "the quality of something that renders it desirable, useful or valuable." It goes on to add, "the quality within a person that renders him or her deserving of respect."

Frankly, we all have different definitions of worth. To a Chicago Cubs fan, seeing the home team win Game Seven of the World Series at Wrigley Field would be priceless. To a life-long Yankees fan, it might just be "another winning season." A long-distance runner might give his eyeteeth to qualify for and run in the Boston Marathon, while for the rest of us it may sound like a very painful, unfulfilling experience.

These subjective valuations of worth vary from person to person. The definition we are seeking is somewhat more tangible, but still elusive.

True worth in the financial arena does not start with assets, money or income. It starts with attitude, desire and ability. I have worked with, or interviewed, hundreds of business owners. I've noticed they have very little in common with each other. What they do have in common is providing value to the world.

Whether it is creating or improving a product offering or an innovative service, almost always there is value delivered to their customers. As a result of creating value for others, many see success in terms of greater income and assets. However, the underlying theme is the fact that all of these entrepreneurs were *cognoscenti* of their worth, not their financial worth, but their *true* worth.

The interesting thing about understanding your worth is that there is no need to focus on money. That is correct—money is irrelevant. Money will come naturally as any good servant to any master.

Google went public some years ago, which immediately made multi-billionaires of the company's founders. Two young men who met at Stanford struck up a friendship and created this very powerful Internet search engine. At the time, a TV special showed one of them driving a mid-size, affordable car, and the other still renting an apartment. Another interesting fact about Google's going public: The founders broke with investment bank community tradition. The newly public shares were offered directly to John and Mary Q. Public—anyone could purchase shares on an equal footing.

These young founders knew their worth. It is not expressed in a balance sheet, but in their purpose of building the best search engine on the planet and allowing all of us to surf the Internet more easily.

Did they decide to make a billion dollars? No, they decided to develop a solution to a problem, and the money flowed to them in the same way that gravity keeps us grounded. They did not set out like many of their Stanford classmates to find a $100,000- or $200,000-per-year job. They set out to provide a service that ultimately became very valuable to all of us.

Their worth is in the idea, the offering and the attitude— intangible ideals that yield tangible results that ultimately yield money—in their case, a vast amount of money.

Should you run out tomorrow and create something new? Maybe or maybe not. Identifying your worth is the first step. A few years ago, we were helping a client obtain financing on a home he was building. He appeared apprehensive about qualifying for a mortgage, even though he had millions of dollars in assets. It became necessary to acquaint him with his True Financial Worth and explain to him that he had grown his estate to a point where he was figuratively a 600-pound gorilla. Any banker would love to have his business, since his ability to pay the loan back was virtually guaranteed.

Financial net worth does not automatically ensure financial success, but it does provide a foundation to take advantage of opportunities—many opportunities.

Most Americans are familiar with real estate mogul Donald Trump. What most Americans don't know is how Donald Trump has, on a couple of occasions, come close to going bankrupt. There were a series of high-interest-rate bank loans that were about to be called due in 1990, after the savings-and-loan debacle. Trump was able to talk his bankers into supporting a plan that reconfigured his debt and saved his real estate empire. Donald Trump knows his worth. It is more than just the assets and liabilities that comprise his balance sheet. A hint of his True Worth can be seen in his distinctive swagger and celebrity persona.

Let's switch gears and look at this question from the eyes of a group of second-semester, fourth-year college students. At this point in time, most of this crop of soon-to-be college graduates are looking for jobs. They are competing for a starting salary that is set by the marketplace, and invariably is insufficient to cover rent and college loan payments. A roommate or two is found to share the rent, utilities and food, in order to make ends meet. Calculators come out and the math is done, which indicates two roommates plus a used car equals a little spending money left over to enjoy a weekend (forget about 401(k) contributions!).

It is a formula. Seems like everyone is doing it. This is life. Accept it and move on.

One of my mentors, Ed Coyle, tells a story about how his grandmother hoped and prayed that he would join the railroad after college so that his income would be secure. Oh, how carefully he avoided telling his grandmother he was selling insurance, for surely nothing would ever become of him then! Personally, I'm certainly grateful he took the road less traveled, paid his dues, started a company, and pursued his True Value.

For some, the railroad job may be the right and true course. But for others, investigating alternatives should be a curriculum requirement. This is soul-searching-type thinking. It is not regimented, comfortable thinking. It feels awkward. There are no rules and no boundaries.

Outside forces do not automatically place a dollar sign on your forehead because you have this or that degree from this or that school.

You have to flip the whole process around and ask one simple question of yourself: What do I love doing and how can I get paid to do it? Is it that simple? *Yes, it is.*

Take "old blue eyes," Frank Sinatra. Would you pay him a million dollars to set up the stage and arrange the back-up orchestra and accoutrements? No. Would you pay him a million dollars to perform his classic songs? Frank Sinatra loved singing and performing, and he found a way to get paid for it. Not initially, though. He had to start off singing in Depression-Era New Jersey nightclubs before World War II. Eventually, success took hold, and off he went doing what he loved to do and getting paid handsomely for it.

Certainly legions of his fans thought his vocal chords were worth a million bucks.

We all know when something is worth the money and when it is not. We vote with our feet and our pocketbooks. Do we choose a cup of coffee for $4 (Starbucks) or $1.50 (local diner)? A bottle of wine for $80 or $8? A luxury car for many thousands or a near-junker for a few hundred? In each of these choices, premium experience motivates us to consider paying substantially more for the same utility.

Worth is defined by something more than the object itself. It is the same with people.

I have the opportunity to interview people from all walks of life on a weekly basis. They all have different life stories. No one is the same. Many times they are not where they want to be. Nor are they aware of dangers lurking on the horizon. My job is to at least make them aware of these realities.

When the banking industry was consolidating in the 1990s, I had the opportunity to discuss these changes with people working in management positions. A few were advised to seek employment in new endeavors, due to pending elimination or outsourcing of their positions. Unfortunately, there were several who needed retraining in a new field, accompanied by a severe cut in pay. The $100,000 or $150,000 job was going away, and their worth and their new position was significantly less.

This is a tough subject to discuss. Over the years, the banking industry, like many before it, had become bloated with bureaucracy and was overpaying these individuals. I'm not saying that these people were not worth their salaries, but new systems and operations had rendered this value obsolete. They just did not know it yet. There was a light at the end of the tunnel, but it was not an opportunity, it was a train racing toward them, called "bank consolidation." They needed to get out of the way, seek retraining, and a new profession.

This is happening, and has been happening, in the manufacturing sector for the past three decades. Maybe that tried-and-true railroad job is not really that secure after all.

Security—job security: What does that mean in the new millennium? After World War II, it meant join the corporate world, work hard for 50 years, and collect the gold watch and pension. Sounds like a fairy tale with a typical "they all lived happily ever after" ending.

The definition of job security has drastically changed. Responsibility for providing security lies squarely on each worker's own shoulders. Yes, you must now provide yourself with job security.

Changing the Conversation

Let's go back to our recently hired college graduates who will be working from now through the middle of the century, and maybe beyond. You think there are more trains heading in their direction? Yes, and emphatically, yes! There will be so many changes we can't possibly imagine. The velocity of this change will continue to increase.

College graduates in 1980 did not have laptops or PCs. College graduates in 1990 did not know how to Google. Graduates in 2000 did not have customized iPod playlists.

The pace of life will only quicken, not slow down. All jobs are becoming specialized. All will have worth, only if they provide special value.

As every large corporation knows, either you are first in your market or you specialize in a niche market. Anything in between gets clobbered. America's middle-manager bankers were downsized, outsourced or eliminated. In manufacturing, unless one specializes in a skill or operates a machine or computer that cannot be commoditized, then one's job is in peril. So what does one do?

One increases one's worth. One's worth to the world. Begin to do what you love doing, and your worth will go up.

The adult education industry has been growing at a rapid rate and is estimated to be one of the fastest-growing industries in the next 20 years. You may have to be re-educated or retrained if your current field of expertise is going the way of the dinosaur. It is all about improving your worth to the world. You are now a corporation of one. As such, you are responsible for production, distribution, marketing, sales, accounting and new product development.

Despite the obsolescence that surrounds us, all businesses require capital and people to perform the tasks and functions that machines and computers are unable to perform. Your mission is to flip the tables and honestly discuss your worth.

Are you a $100,000 middle-management banker whose value is diminishing? What is it that you are uniquely good at doing? If you do not have a skill or an avocation that you can market, go out and develop one. It does not have to be an Internet search engine worth billions to the world, but rather a skill sufficiently marketable to satisfy your economic needs.

Changing the Conversation

Money will follow naturally once you begin bringing value to the table.

The key to economic freedom requires flipping the old model upside down. You call the shots and write your own business plan, then the world seeks you out for the value you deliver.

Every employee hired in our firm is told we recognize that they are in charge!...but...only if they step up, accept personal accountability, and prove this to be true.

Conversely...their lacking this core understanding becomes their biggest liability, their greatest enemy, their largest stumbling block to increasing their worth and preventing their obsolescence.

Consider changing the definition of self worth to the essence of who you are and what you bring to society. The financial side of the equation will come naturally, as money is always attracted to people of substance. For young people, this is a must. Break out of the old mold before you become too fixed in this old way of thinking.

Everyone possesses skills that come very easily to them. When finding their groove, people perform their unique dance effortlessly, while the rest of us marvel.

Unfortunately, many people never practice these skills for the rest of us to enjoy, but remain stuck in jobs undertaken out of deemed necessity or perceived insecurity.

Increase your worth by eliminating obstacles and past-based thinking. Concentrate on what you love. Keep your eyes open to new opportunities to apply your expertise and create solutions for others.

It is in this way that you will discover your True Worth.

Whose Property Do You Own?

Several years ago I met with an elderly gentleman and his wife about their estate plan. They were contemplating some changes. When the wife asked what would happen to their property after their deaths, the husband blurted out, "Don't sell any of my things until I've been dead and buried for two weeks!"

We all laughed, but there was a subtle point to his emotional outburst. His possessions were very important to him. He did not want anyone to touch any of his things until it was absolutely certain he wasn't coming back.

Comedian George Carlin had a routine years ago about "stuff." My stuff is great, is valuable; your stuff is junk (although he used a more colorful term!).

He's right. We really do become very attached to our stuff. Our stuff is who we are. We are identified by the car we drive, the clothes we wear, and homes we live in.

Museums are great places to explore our history's "back stories" by viewing pictures and artifacts. On one visit, I came upon a satirical painting of Native Americans selling Manhattan Island to the Dutch—the famous "$24 dollars of trinkets" real estate trade. Recall that Peter Minuit—to legally safeguard the settlers' investments, possessions and farms in what was to become Nieuw Amsterdam—"purchased" Manhattan from the Mannahatta branch of the Lenape Indians. Actually, the purchase price was 60 guilders of trade goods, worth about $1,000 in today's dollars.

Why do I mention this painting? What caught my eye were the expressions on the Lenape Indians' faces. The chief accepting payment had a slight smirk on his face. The Indians standing behind him, gesturing toward the Dutch settlers, portrayed disbelief that Europeans were actually "paying" for the island. What's more—another group of Indians behind the first group were actually laughing!

Why were the Indians in this museum painting laughing? Our first instinct, due to our cultural perspective, is to view this scene as an example of the Indians' extreme naïveté. But after further reflection, I submit the Indians truly understood the concept of ownership: It doesn't exist. "Purchase" to them was really a shrewd combination of rental agreement and treaty or alliance between two groups. New York's Manhattan Island, with its division into smaller and smaller parcels over past centuries, has resulted in it now being "owned" by many thousands of people—virtually none of them related to the original settlers. Centuries from now, history will repeat itself yet again.

Ownership of property is simply our way of turning the abstract into something concrete. While real estate is tangible (it can be seen, utilized and enjoyed), stocks, bonds, bank accounts and insurance policies are intangible—not something we can get our arms around.

Either way, we cannot take any of it with us.

Ownership of property by the masses has occurred only in recent history. For most of humanity's existence on this planet, property ownership was reserved for kings, royalty and a select number of merchants.

There is a Broadway play that has been around for many years called "Spamalot." It's a send-up satire based on

British comedy troupe Monty Python's motion picture "Monty Python and the Holy Grail." The plot involves the mythical King Arthur and his Knights of the Roundtable and their search for the Holy Grail. There is a particular scene where King Arthur asks for directions from two serfs who are covered in mud, working in a field, while curiously engaged in a highly sophisticated political discussion. It is a satire on the feudal system.

Picture a serf stacking piles of earthen sod, meanwhile offering the trenchant comment, "Pulling a sword from a stone is no foundation for a system of government!" The gist of the two serfs' governmental dialogue: The king inherits the throne solely because he was born of royalty and we serfs are indentured servants of the king until we die.

I can still hear the second serf's protest: "How did he become king? I didn't vote for him."

It is quite a comical scene viewed from a 21st century democratic point of view. The common man, the serf, was not entitled to rights of ownership and simply was expected to be happy to die a natural death in serfdom rather than being jailed or killed for attempting to improve his position.

Changing the Conversation

Today we take property ownership very personally. What we fail to see is that property does not die—it simply passes from person to person. We are more like stewards and custodians, rather than owners—since our ownership is temporary and based on our life expectancy and that of our heirs if the property stays "in the family."

A funny bumper sticker that has been around awhile states, "I'm spending my kid's inheritance." We can chuckle at this humor, but there is a point to be made: It is okay to spend the earnings on our money *and* the principal.

Now, before you write me off as a loony or burn me at the stake for financial heresy, consider both sides of the story.

Indeed there's a school of thought taught by a good majority of financial and accounting professionals that commands: "Never spend any principal."

We would agree—spending principal is not generally a good thing. In certain circles it may even be considered criminal. There once was an elderly gentleman who went to his doctor for his annual physical. After the tests were completed, the doctor said, "I have good news and I have bad news. The good news is you're as strong as a horse and will live for at least another 10 years. The bad news is, I was just on the phone with your financial advisor and he says you're going to run out of money next year."

The fear most retirees have is that their money won't last—that they will be a burden to their family or wind up destitute on the street. At our firm, we tend to adhere to the conservative party line of planning for our clients, and stress the avoidance of spending down principal.

However, there are times when exceptions are warranted.

Earlier I mentioned that in 1980 my elderly grandfather moved in with my parents. His health was failing and my grandmother was having a hard time taking care of him. My grandparents owned savings accounts and some CDs when they came to live with my parents. Fifteen years later, after both had passed, the balances in their accounts were basically the same. That upstanding, proud, frugal generation of Americans didn't touch their principal!

When my family gets together during the holidays, our conversations frequently turn to reminiscences of our grandparents. We retell stories and talk about their lives and the impact that their lives have had on all of us. We never discuss their bank accounts and CDs that they left for us. We don't talk about the home they lived in until 1980, nor do we talk about any other property they owned. While my dad still has my grandfather's shotgun (which is used occasionally for hunting), the discussion of their property never comes up.

Rather, who they were, what they stood for, and their living memory are what is retold and remembered. We have pictures of our grandparents and their parents and their parents, but I have yet to find a listing of property owned by any of them.

Reflecting now, my grandparents could have spent some of their principal on trips with their children and grandchildren, perhaps imparting more wisdom along the way. Instead, they stayed home and saved—"for a rainy day." There are many things they could have done with at least a portion of their savings, which would have further enriched their lives while also strengthening their legacies. Now, I'm not suggesting one should start spending money willy-nilly—*perish the thought!* But you should consider what it is you are holding onto so tightly.

I'm reminded of a saying that illustrates the power that property has over us: "The king fears the man who stands before him with no need." It is a very profound statement. During feudal times, the serf could have rebelled against the "indentured servant equals food and shelter" formula. He could have repudiated the system of property rights and refused to become a slave to the system. Arguably he could have lived off the land and put himself out for hire.

When you think about it, a feudal system of property rights still exists today. The difference: The king has been replaced by consumerism. We can do without three TVs, three-car garages, three personal phones, and on and on. We choose to "own" these extras because it makes life easier and more enjoyable.

Money can't buy happiness, but it makes the journey more comfortable. So, are you controlling the money or is the money controlling you?

Property and money can attach themselves to us and our psyche. Releasing that attachment and mastering property is the key to financial peace of mind. Some day in the future, your children and grandchildren will be discussing the impact you had on their lives, without mentioning property. Do you have a death grip on your property or is it enriching your life and the lives of those around you?

There are many among us who collect property for the sake of gathering more property. There's often an insatiable appetite for more and more. There is never enough. As the old saw goes, "The one with the most toys at the end wins."

Fortunately, this group of people represents only about 5% of the population, as determined in many high-net-worth surveys. A majority of us just wants to have enough money to live comfortably, with a little cushion.

The question is, when is enough *enough*? There is a point in time, if you are fortunate, when you move from the "get rich" business to the "stay rich" business. We refer to these people as wealthy, or high net worth.

The interesting part is, most people who are now in the "stay rich" business think that they are still in the "get rich" business. They have been so busy accumulating and growing assets for tomorrow, they haven't really given any attention to the fact that tomorrow is *today*. This is not unusual. After all, they've spent the majority of their adult lives trying to accumulate assets. Old habits and mindsets, we all know, are very hard to break.

Shouldn't property ownership take on a different meaning at this point? Wealthy families will probably never need to spend a penny of their capital, so property takes on a life of its own. Yes, that is correct; property begins to grow at a rate that is above the level needed to maintain a strong cash flow stream sufficient to meet family needs. Why is this important? All too often, people in this position still apply the "get rich" approach and still hold tightly to their property as well as their surplus income.

Bill Gates began a foundation in 1994 at the age of 39, funding it with $94 million. He has continued to fund this foundation over the past decade to a current balance of $27 billion. The Bill and Melinda Gates Foundation is an example of "letting go" of property to place it in use for future generations. At a young age, Bill Gates realized his legacy was not only to put a computer in every home, but also to help the children of the world. Bill and Melinda Gates currently have three children who will most likely be profoundly affected by their parents' use of family property.

As parents and grandparents, we want to bequeath several things to family members—a strong work ethic, motivation and aspiration, a humble respect for the dignity of daily labor. We are compelled continually to preach to our children, as Bill Gates did as a guest speaker at a high school graduation, "Flipping burgers is not beneath your dignity." Our grandparents had a different word for burger flipping—they called it "opportunity."

That said—we also want our children to lead happy lives without the constant, nagging worry concerning their financial security.

As mentioned earlier, after learning and earning, we begin to *yearn*. I like to think of the yearning phase as the most productive. It is during this stage that we can make the biggest impact on future generations. We are now in a position where we can impart our wisdom in perhaps more toned-down fashion, as we are further removed from the dual pressures of earning a buck and raising a family. We can practice what I like to call "kind management," where we can help our children and grandchildren (or causes we believe in) surmount their bumps. Help them with what they need, not necessarily with what they want. Help lead them by personal example, demonstrating that our financial accomplishments in life do not define us.

Each person's legacy can be passed on through the sharing

of time, talent or treasure. Are you beginning to question how you treat your property? Do you have white-knuckled hands grasping it with all your might? There are many ways to release this energy for the greater use it can achieve. We can't be as generous as the Gates, but we certainly can begin to work and use our stuff differently.

In hindsight, if that funny museum painting is correct, the laughing, duplicitous, wise Lenape Indians of early 17th century Manhattan Island had a very healthy appreciation of what property, possessions and resources are really about. Land—and, by extension, other forms of property—remain long after we're gone, though they must be stewarded and used during our lives, then left in better shape for future generations. Along the way, they can provide a sense of security to allow us to focus on the things that really matter.

We're Better Together

Recently I scheduled a trip to the West Coast to visit a client. My plane was to depart from Chicago's O'Hare Airport at 9 a.m., arriving in Los Angeles at 11:05 a.m. My meeting was slated for 4 p.m.—plenty of slack time in the schedule, or so I thought.

My cell phone rang at 6:45 a.m. with a message from Orbitz alerting that my flight had been canceled due to mechanical problems. I immediately called reservations and was told I was on standby for a 10:05 a.m. flight, with no seats available yet. So to be safe, Orbitz encouraged me to reserve a seat on the next flight out with open seats, not leaving until day's end, 6 p.m. Surely I could fly out of Chicago way before then, I thought! But I took the precaution of booking the dinnertime flight.

As I waited, I noticed the airport was unusually busy for a Friday morning, and soon discovered it was the start of spring break for Chicago schools. I stood for 45 minutes in a crowded, shoulder-to-shoulder line, finally making my way to the reservation desk, and was placed on standby for the 10:05 flight—No. 46 on the list. *My day was getting worse and worse.* I began to feel anxious and could feel my blood pressure start to rise. As the day went on, I was placed on standby for the next flight out, No. 32. —And the next flight, No. 26. —And then the next flight, No. 34. By mid-afternoon I had to call my client and say, "I think I'll be very late. Are you okay with a late dinner?" Then the crowd really started to get to me. I was hot and sweaty and angry at the airline for not having a contingency plan. *I hate to be late!* In retrospect, that early-morning decision to book the 6 p.m. flight really paid off. I was able to finally meet my client for a 9:30 p.m. dinner in California and fell into bed by 1 a.m.—exhausted. It had been a long, stressful day!

Air travel is certainly not easy these days. Who doesn't have their own missed-flight horror story ending in elevated blood pressure, indigestion or a tension headache? Stress affects us physically. Short-term, it can cause minor discomfort; long-term, chronic disease and even death.

Canadian endocrinologist Hans Selye first linked stress and health in the 1930s. He was the first to use the word *stress,* previously an engineering term, to explain what happens to us as we cope with unexpected and difficult changes in our lives. Selye discovered a direct link between the stress hormone cortisol and long-term effects on the health of rats. Cortisol is key to the stress-illness connection. When we perceive danger, our adrenaline glands secrete cortisol, which in turn increases our heart rate, breathing and glucose blood levels—facilitating a fight-or-flight reaction.

These physical changes prepare our body to respond to a threat in our environment. In order to focus energy on this protective response, cortisol also shuts down digestion, reproduction, physical growth and other parts of our immune system. When the threat passes, cortisol levels begin to lower, taking 40-60 minutes, and our body begins to function normally again. This natural response is necessary and may cause some sweating or nausea. Constant elevated cortisol levels, however, can lead to serious health problems such as heart disease, depression, intestinal problems, gum disease, adult-onset diabetes, arthritis and even cancer.

The challenge, then, is how to deal with stress in our daily lives. We can't eliminate frustration. We don't have control over the airlines, the weather, our work or a bad stock market. But we can control the way we respond when challenged.

The answer lies in finding healthy ways to cope—by accommodating and adapting rather than becoming overwhelmed.

We can improve our chance for good health by adjusting our expectations. If we build a large block of flex time into our travel schedule, we will avoid becoming stressed out and miserable in O'Hare Airport with 10,000 of our closest friends.

We all know that good nutrition, regular exercise and adequate sleep are also vital to good health. So is there anything else we should consider? Yes. *Connectivity*—connecting with family, friends, coworkers, organizations, our country and the world. A healthy social life is good for the body, too.

Last year my wife and I vacationed at an Arizona spa with another couple and their father, Walter. Walter is 78 years old and recently widowed. Walter enjoyed every minute of his week with us. Each meal found him at a different table meeting new people and making new friends. He also was an eager participant in all scheduled activities, excited to learn anything new, asking questions like an inquisitive eight-year-old boy. Walter sought out new information and new friends each day. He made many new connections that week, which will no doubt add to his circle of friends.

There's another 78 year old I know. He is married and lives with his wife in a rural area in the East. Each day, day in and day out, he has the same routine. He eats his three meals in the kitchen, putters around the house a little, sits in front of the TV, and naps each afternoon. He will go out to eat and take short trips when his wife earnestly implores him to do so. He does not like having his routine altered in any way. He just seems to be waiting in place. He seems to be following the same pattern as his father, who died at age 89—yes, definitely a good life, but with surprising little social connectivity during his latter years.

This 78 year old is my dear dad. He and Walter are worlds apart. Many scientific studies have shown that Walter's way is the far better way to live and thrive.

A study has found that women belonging to breast cancer support groups have a 40% higher survival rate than women who do not participate. Another study has found that widowed men with prior strong spousal relationships, but few close friends, are much more likely to experience deep depression upon losing their wives than men with a strong social network.

Let's face it: No man is an island. We are social beings. We need family, friends and social activities to ease stress and maintain good health.

Personal connections motivate us. They are critical to our psychological well-being. Politicians understand this and use it to their advantage. Presidential candidates feverishly try to attract more voters during the primary season. They hold rallies and deliver speeches to community groups, workers and party faithful in an effort to reach the American people.

Since 1960, candidates have enjoyed great political success by understanding and embracing technology that creates a positive, personal connection with potential voters. The televised Kennedy-Nixon debates made a huge impact on that election. Nixon appeared rigid, stoic, didactic and tired contrasted to Kennedy's natural charisma, charm, fresh energy and good looks. JFK's TV image made him more personally appealing to voters.

Changing the Conversation

During the 2008 primaries, Barack Obama and Hillary Clinton held rallies days apart in Houston. Clinton's rally attracted 5,000 Texas voters. Obama addressed a crowd of 20,000 younger supporters the next day. His rally exceeded Clinton's by 15,000—but why? It was a very closely run primary race between the two of them. The "why" is personal connection. Obama contacted the maximum number of potential voters by using the newest technology—cell phone text-messaging and Internet blogs. In this way, he attracted young people as far as a five-hour drive away. Obama reached out and touched individual voters, and it paid off. He achieved great fundraising success with this strategy as well.

Connectivity promotes physical well-being as well as interpersonal success. We play an important part in each other's lives. Whether by common heritage, political affiliation or national citizenry, we are in relationships and thereby need to support each other.

Whether you agree or disagree with America's military policy, we all concur that our soldiers, sailors and airmen should receive our validation and support. They serve our country, and today are in harm's way in Iraq, Afghanistan and around the globe. World conflicts have spread our military very thin. As a result, the National

Guard and Reserve have been called up for active duty for periods of 12-24 months.

Several years ago, some retired military officers and senior enlisted non-commissioned officers organized to form USA Cares. This volunteer organization helps families of active-duty guardsmen and reservists negotiate and pay their bills. What many of us don't realize—when these members of the civilian sector are called to duty, they may take a very large pay cut from their civilian jobs. The reduced military pay scales leave them financially exposed, unable to meet their mortgages or pay bills. USA Cares helps negotiate lower bills and deferred payments, and in some cases pays expenses to help these military families while their loved ones serve our country.

Philanthropy and a willingness to help others in need are far more common in America than anywhere else in the world. As a citizenry, we like to connect and help, whether it be through social activities, political affiliations, religious groups or charitable organizations.

Such giving—along with physical exercise, continual learning, sound planning and an active network of social relationships—acts to smooth our way along life's journey.

Pass It On

The Bob Marshall Wilderness straddles the Continental Divide in northwestern Montana. If you find yourself there, you should hike up to Sun Butte for a breathtaking vista, miles and miles of beautiful pine forest. When you climb back down to the Sun River bottom, though, your view is quite different. The expansive horizon of trees is replaced with caves carved into rock faces, sulfur hot springs—maybe even a grizzly bear or bighorn sheep.

Down here, the expression springs to mind: *You can't see the forest for the trees.*

These wise words are instructive. What you see depends on your vantage point, what you are looking at, and how closely you're looking. Which "new" or "next" is better? Earlier, I mentioned that when I meet with a family for the first time, I like to see the forest—the Big Picture.

It is important to understand what they value as a family, before delving into the details about money. Money is just a tool, a material good that will take care of itself *provided* that one puts the right "first things first." Begin with an honest examination about what's truly important to you and your family. Intelligently map out how to best position one's self and one's family.

First things first. Family leadership that provides this focus is a critical component of future success.

Just how critical is family leadership? Perhaps an analogy to the properties of water might provide us with some answers. We all know that temperature changes dramatically affect water. Water can assume three states: solid (ice), gas (steam) and liquid. When water is frozen, nothing happens; the status quo rules. Steam is very chaotic, fast-moving and haphazard. But in the liquid state, water is life-giving and fluid.

These three physical states of water analogously remind us of the "rags to riches to rags" scenario. The wealthy first generation is liquid, providing dynamic growth and positive change. The second generation is frozen, neither growing nor dying, just existing in a squandering state. The third generation is chaotic and spendthrift, unable to make good financial decisions. Needless to say, poor money management can cause great heartbreak. I have seen some sad life examples of family devastation that could have been routinely avoided with proper leadership. Here are two of them.

Remember the story about the pilot who died on the day of his retirement? My story continues with his family. His wife was devastated, but financially in good shape. Then the five children, all independent adults, began to request and/or demand that mom provide them with money from the family nest egg. One received money to purchase a home, another to buy an auto repair shop, a third for expensive private high schools and colleges. Mom was a complete pushover. She never handled money before and could not say "no." Within three years of her husband's death, she doled out $1 million to her children. In the fourth year, she sold her house, bought a house with one of her daughters in the Southwest, and moved into the master suite. Even for the next three years, her children hounded her for money. She obliged. Finally, seven years after her husband's death, with $12,000 left, she died of medical complications. She had spent almost 18 months out of the final three years of her life in hospitals, until her death at age 66. A disquieting, tragic story.

A few years later, another woman came to me in a very distressed state. She was a single mother, in her late 40s. She had buried her mother six months earlier, after being her primary caregiver the prior five years. Her older brother had handled all her mother's finances. After her mom's death, she approached her brother to discuss splitting their mom's assets. Her brother surprised her, saying the mom had left all the family assets to him— about $4 million. She was dumbfounded. After months of estate checking, and continued evasions by her brother, she finally examined her mother's will. She was to inherit one-half of the estate. She approached her brother again. He again surprised her, saying that all assets had been placed in joint tenancy with him and their mother six months before her death. He had legal right to all $4 million. She was now completely destroyed, not only by her brother swindling her out of her inheritance, but also by the fact that her mother had never discussed any of the money decisions with her. As close as mother and daughter had always been, her mom inexplicably had allowed herself to be deceived by her son. Life-long memories and relationships with both her mother and brother were now shattered.

Changing the Conversation

These stories could have ended far more happily if each family member had considered the Big Picture—what was important for the entire family. Just as water is profoundly altered by its temperature environment, so, too, are families profoundly impacted by the unchecked transformation of "liquid to ice to steam."

We Baby Boomers and our parents must address the Big Picture, make fundamental shifts in perspective, sooner than later. Now, maybe you are thinking this sounds like Mission Impossible. But it is more like Mission Must. Some of us still have 20 to 40 years, plenty of time, but *tempus fugit!* Now, right now, is the time to consider how to pass on beliefs and values that will ensure our wealth will continue to enhance and sustain lives.

We can make these fundamental changes in three ways: The first and most important shift is one of perspective. That is—we need to see our essential role in affecting change. We need to be strong, effective leaders.

The Judeo-Christian adage says that "to whom much is given, much is expected"; "with great gifts come great responsibility." In my work life, I continually meet business owners and executives, many of whom display remarkable understanding and commitment to growing and developing employees' skills and natural talents. When they discuss this nurturing of human gifts, they are surprisingly humble.

Still, a business is not a family. The fast-paced business world is guided by a quarter-to-quarter focus on productivity and financial performance. Many family leaders, though, must consider a 20-to-40-year perspective on how choices will affect succeeding generations.

The North American Iroquois tribes make all tribal council decisions with an eye to this wisdom. Even today, they begin their tribal gatherings with a reminder that decisions should be finalized *only* after considering the consequences to the Iroquois nation seven generations out—just as their ancestors did seven generations before them. They recognize they all have different agendas that they bring to the tribal lodge.

All of us—it's simply human nature—have short-term objectives. These may arise out of immediate desires, our egos, fractured relationships with other family members, or simply because we believe our agenda is superior and should be implemented. However, by exercising the discipline to focus seven generations into the future, the Iroquois insist on placing seemingly important issues in proper perspective. Now—seven generations is a lot! But just think about the benefits of this long-range view for our great-grandchildren, their kids, and their kids, and their kids! The Iroquois embrace their role as leaders very seriously. They value future tribal well-being over everything else.

One very important step that I see successful multigenerational families take is the figurative "passing of the torch." The first generation may have pulled themselves up by their bootstraps and created a very nice estate. Yet their method of growing their wealth with the skills and tools they used are much different than what the next generation will need to do.

Again—it's human nature—it's difficult to let go. It is very hard to step back out of the limelight. After a lifetime of hard work, it is hard to humble oneself.

Do understand, though—unsuccessful families have all tried to force their agenda on the next generation. But the next generation has a different outlook, will be successful in a different way, with different skills in a different world. By stepping back and handing the reins to the next generation, we avoid the shirtsleeves-to-shirtsleeves scenario in three generations.

Responsible family leadership that values human capital over financial capital is the first behavioral change needed to pass down principles, along with our wealth. .

But how do we lead? What are our guiding principles?

We will know where to begin if we make a second important change—one that expands our time horizon. The second change is more than a change of perspective. It is a change in outlook—how we perceive life and living.

Plain and simple, our time line needs to expand significantly. The critical ingredients required for this expansion are a sense of child-like wonderment and a keen focus on new growth potential.

Some retirees, unfortunately, revert to the dictionary definition of *retirement*—to go away, depart, withdraw from business or public life, fall back, retreat. Too often, we stand helplessly by, witnessing their destructive mental, physical and spiritual mindsets. Human existence is about growth or death. There is no in-between. You are either growing or dying. Simply giving up is to end up on the other side of the grass more quickly and with far less grace and dignity. Being in a state of child-like wonderment, focused on growth and possibility, keeps our minds active, our will strong, our physical stamina intact, and our spiritual life vibrant. Thus, we will be properly equipped to guide our children and grandchildren.

Strong leaders who are earnestly focused on growth and human capital—on their family progeny present and future—will keep family inheritances intact for future generations.

But one more thing must be considered—a third fundamental change: personal habits.

As the old saying goes, "The devil is in the details." Previously, we reviewed KASH, an acronym for Knowledge, Attitude, Skills and Habits. Generally, knowledge and a good attitude help to develop the skills needed to change habits. Maybe you want to be around to see your fifth generation born and raised. Well, you'll have to live to be at least 100 for that, the good Lord willing. Recent medical advances have actually made this a possibility. However, this depends on how you live your life.

Drs. Mehmet C. Oz and Michael F. Roizen discussed their book, *You: Staying Young* (2007), on "The Oprah Winfrey Show." The book describes how to live physically, mentally and spiritually, if you want to reach 100 with a high quality of life. On "Oprah!," the authors tested 100 audience members to determine if their lifestyles would afford them a high probability of living to age 100. Only one woman scored a high enough score, based on her daily habits.

She explained her regimen: First thing each morning, she goes to a health-fitness club with a friend and spends an hour doing aerobic exercises. Additionally, she does weight lifting several times a week. Also, she meditates daily to calm her mind and focus on each day ahead. She enjoys a large social network. She avoids fast food, preparing most of her meals at home.

Now—all of us understand the wisdom behind this woman's regimen. But how many people have changed their attitudes and developed the skills necessary to make needed changes a daily habit? It all starts with KASH. There's no easy solution.

There's still time for nearly everyone to change one's leadership perspective, one's time horizon, one's personal habits. If we act, we can help our children and grandchildren be wise custodians of their inheritance. By many estimates, there will be $14 trillion-to-$41 trillion worth of assets inherited by Baby Boomers over the next 40 years. It's also estimated that there are approximately five million Americans with assets over $1 million, excluding their homes. We have grown into a very affluent nation without the prerequisites to deal with such enormous financial capital.

Our responsibility lies in looking beyond a short-term, quarter-to-quarter business viewpoint—focusing instead on at least two generations ahead. Projecting out 20 to 40 years can offer a much greater clarity and range of vision, and bring a certain peace of mind.

Standing atop a high Montana butte, one's view is not blocked by individual conifers or interrupted by the daily animal survival rituals in the valley below.

The horizon up here appears beautiful and infinite.

Mentoring and teaching the next generations—moving ahead with a sound plan and purpose—these are the actions that place caring, love, generosity, human capital, money and property in the best possible position to continue supporting all of one's family endeavors.

What 'To Live' Really Means

I met Margaret 15 years ago. She changed my outlook on life. She was not a teacher, public speaker or best-selling author. It wasn't her words that moved me, but her countenance, her spirit, her vital connection to the importance of living each day in the present with immense joy and great purpose.

Margaret had what others would consider an extremely unfair and difficult life. Her first husband died of a heart attack, her second of colon cancer. Her three sons died of AIDS in the beginning, middle and end of the 1980s. Her daughter abandoned her two children in the mid-1980s, leaving Margaret to raise them on her own. About the time I met her, she was facing the first of three cancers that eventually took her sight and parts of several major organs.

In the last few years of her life, I drove to her home to

visit her and discuss her life and finances. The house was dark. Being blind, she did not require lights. Her living room was adorned with pictures of her family, most of them deceased. Yet her face bestowed an angelic look at all times, radiating peace and joy. When I asked her how she was doing, she responded she was happy to be alive.

When I asked her how she was able to cope with all of the tragedy in her life, along with her current bout of medical issues, she responded simply, "I say a prayer before I go to bed each night, and ask God to keep me safe. When I awake in the morning, I thank God for the new day that is presented to me."

So profound! So real! So true—but so hard for most of us to see as we focus on our aches and pains, dysfunctional family members, and the troubles of the world. To this day, I know Margaret has profoundly altered my view of life for the better.

So what does Margaret's story say to you? How can she possibly be so happy being dealt a dreadfully unlucky hand in life? Maybe it's true that our Maker only gives us what we can handle? Maybe not? Perhaps you have been feeling, like I have over the past couple tumultuous years, that nothing is certain except maybe death and taxes.

As we automatically consume more and more with the years rolling by, we probably haven't given much thought to the haves and have-nots. Here I am not measuring in terms of dollars, but in terms of great joy, fulfillment and happiness.

Has anyone among us recently experienced the fear of losing all of our worldly possessions? Sure—virtually everyone has confronted that demon. I know my wife and I discussed our situation during the market-upheaval days of September 2008. Ultimately, we pledged to each other we would be okay—no matter what.

Money, possessions, material things of all varieties may hold an icy grip on each one of us during challenging times. Too often we convince ourselves that all our "stuff" is absolutely necessary—that we can't live without it. Fear consumes us. We become afraid we won't be able to acquire our wants and desires. We become afraid we will lose things we already own. Either way, we tend to freeze and take no action. As individuals, families, the country and the world, this ominous icy grip that we feel has paralyzed the planet time and time again.

Margaret instinctively understood that "to live" means to embrace every day without fear of losing one's possessions—or one's life. If we would delude ourselves that we can stay removed from the world on our island or in our cave, then let me again note Thomas Friedman's cautionary 2005 book, *The World Is Flat*. He emphasizes that we are all connected. The Internet, cellular phones and all things digital have connected all of us.

During the 2008-2009 global economic crisis, "currency swaps" between nations, executed in mere seconds, kept money moving around the globe to prevent local "runs on banks." Finances are now global—not parochial. The same goes for geopolitics. And so it is as well for all things "non-financial."

Recently, I attended a speech presented by Boston College's Dr. Paul Schervish, a sociology professor and director of the school's Center on Wealth and Philanthropy. He defines "world philanthropy" today as "global, spiritual citizenship."

When we practice philanthropy, we first visualize what it means to us personally. We internalize its importance and believe in it. This is not about charity. Charity is mostly about check writing. Philanthropy is about essence and being—commitment to our fellow human beings. If charity is an egg—philanthropy is the chicken.

The former may show occasional involvement, but the latter demonstrates ongoing commitment.

Many times we are asked to contribute to one cause or another. Out of obligation or friendship, we write a check. One wealthy philanthropist whom I know harshly terms this the "spray and pray" method of charity. If you are like me, you periodically give thought to dropping a dollar into a panhandler's cup and quickly moving on. It's much harder to pause and question panhandlers who say they need money for food, then walk them to a nearby restaurant and buy their breakfast.

Now, I'm probably as cynical as you—aren't many panhandlers simply fleecing us out of our hard-earned money? It's hard, seeing panhandlers daily on the streets, not to become numb to the presence of those in need. No judgment here of you and me—just of our human nature to avoid the nastiness of life.

Philanthropy was passed down to us by a Founding Father, Benjamin Franklin. The last of his $2.2 million foundation was distributed to the City of Philadelphia in 1989. It's virtually impossible to drive around this City of Brotherly Love without stumbling upon many of the institutions that have benefited from Ben

Franklin's foundation.

Fellow "robber barons" John D. Rockefeller and Andrew Carnegie each established huge philanthropic causes that remain with us today. I clearly recall walking into my local library in the 1960s, passing beneath the Carnegie name etched on the Romanesque portico. The Rockefeller Foundation, today with assets of $3.3 billion, was established in 1913 to "promote the well-being" of humanity.

What all three philanthropists were espousing—what Warren Buffett and Bill and Melinda Gates and other philanthropists are practicing today—springs from our souls' desire to help our fellow man. It is all about the money (Franklin, Rockefeller, Carnegie, et al.). It is not about the money at all (Margaret).

You see, in Margaret's case, it was all about her loved ones. Her philanthropy of caring for her sick family members and spreading joy to everyone she met was very valuable to the world.

This is where each of us can start. We don't need a lot of money, because our time and our talents are just as valuable, and many times more valuable than our money.

About 10 years ago, a couple I know were going through pre-retirement planning, trying to decide what they were going to do with the rest of their lives. With their three daughters grown and married, Len and Rose felt moved to give back to society in some way. They decided to spend three years teaching in a rural school in a very poor, undeveloped area of our country. They landed in a private school near a remote Indian reservation in northern New Mexico. Conditions were far less than optimal. A small house was offered to them, with none of the creature comforts (no drinkable water, phone, cable, air conditioning, etc.). They worked very hard for three years, trying to break the cycle of poor education, drug and alcohol abuse, and welfare entitlement that had settled onto the reservation.

Many stories of accomplishments emerged from those first three years. In 2008, they decided to return. Len is the new school principal, and Rose is the Title I and kindergarten teacher. They volunteer their services with little pay in the same tough living conditions. Theirs is a story of amazing work and complete dedication to under-privileged American youth.

There are so many more poignant stories of people whom

we know doing unusual, astonishing, awe-inspiring, be-wildering, random acts of kindness: Helping a battered wife and her three children get a fresh start, or providing pain-relief massages for severe-burn victims. This is phi-lanthropy at its finest—not necessarily demanding a lot of money, but certainly a wealth of time and effort.

Little things make all the difference. A gentleman I met recently had vacationed in India 15 years ago with his family. At the time, he lived in Mexico City. During the trip, they passed through Calcutta. He had made a commitment to himself years earlier—if he ever visit-ed India, he would personally deliver a $100 check to Mother Teresa's Missionaries of Charity mission. After wandering around Calcutta a few hours, after being giv-en wrong directions, he finally found the mission. He walked up, knocked on the door, waited a few moments, then a kindly young nun opened the door. He tried to communicate that he was making a donation and handed over the check. The young nun took the check, thanked him, then closed the door. Feeling a bit unful-filled, he knocked on the door again. The young nun again opened the door, with a puzzled look. He hesi-tantly explained that he'd like to come in for a few min-utes to visit. She motioned him to take a seat and wait for her to return. A few minutes passed. The young nun returned with Mother Teresa!

Mother Teresa had a notebook and was writing out a receipt to give him. Apparently, the young nun thought this American needed proof of his gift and was attempting to comply with his request.

For several minutes, Mother Teresa graciously visited with him. At the end of their conversation, she asked him for a favor. She asked that he visit one of the Mexico City missions and take a message to the sisters at the mission that Mother Teresa was praying for them daily.

He happily complied. He visited the mission a few weeks after his return home. This time when he knocked on the door, a very frustrated sister answered. As he relayed the message to this impatient nun, he quickly saw that she was at her wits' end. Just as he arrived, one of the mission's boys had vomited in the hallway. The mission was currently very short-staffed, so the sister handed him a mop and bucket to clean up the mess. He spent the next few hours helping out around the mission after cleaning up the first mess. Returning home, he suddenly realized he was much more fulfilled by this visit than even meeting Mother Teresa.

Sometimes all that is needed is someone to pitch in and clean up a mess.

Socrates insisted that "the unexamined life is not worth living." So, too, must our wealth—in money, time, abilities and goods of this earth—be put to use in such a way that we discover their greater worth and live fulfilled in accordance with that meaning.

Dr. Schervish made another very telling point concerning "formal" philanthropy. *Formal* refers more to charity, as defined earlier. He feels that his life work will not be finished until all formal philanthropy is erased from the earth! Only when we recast our thinking in beneficial and ethical terms—see ourselves as the active stewards, managers and doers of our philanthropy—will we then practice true philanthropy.

I'm absolutely humbled and in awe of all the people I meet who do good works without complaint, without remorse, without any expectation of a *quid pro quo* other than the sheer happiness that shines from their eyes. Whether you are a Warren Buffett, or a Len and Rose, or a Margaret, or someone dedicated to any other gifting, philanthropy is what you make of it. Keep writing the gifting checks—money used effectively can move mountains. But don't forget to put down the pen and pick up a mop and bucket.

Arguably one of the greatest philanthropists of all time was St. Francis of Assisi (1182-1226), whose words may guide us all: "Lord, make me an instrument of your peace." His famous prayer advocated sowing things—love, pardon, faith, hope, light and joy. He thought it far better to be proactive—to console, to understand, to love, to give, to pardon, to transition after an active life to a Heavenly eternity.

Regardless of your spiritual or religious affiliation, these words offer us peace of mind, especially during our recent trying times.

When giving to others, our hope is revealed. When giving to others, our true self is discovered. When giving to others without expectation of anything in return, we become clear about our higher purpose on this earth…and that is the essence of philanthropy.

Growing Greatness

Each time the holidays roll around, I'm reminded of an old plumber story that my boss Ed Coyle used to tell.

It was New Year's Eve. A couple living in a posh condo in downtown Chicago was preparing to receive friends and family for a New Year's Eve party. An hour before guests were due, the hostess discovered their toilets were backed up. No functioning commode—and thirsty, hungry guests were on the way. Panic set in! Quickly, the couple searched the Yellow Pages for plumbers, and after repeated tries, reached a plumber closing up shop. They pleaded with him to fix their broken toilet.

The plumber came, looked around for a few minutes, banged on a pipe, and the toilets began working again. Evening saved! The party was a great success, and in early January the plumber's bill arrived: $225. The couple was astounded! He was five minutes away from their condo and spent maybe five minutes fixing the backed-up toilet. They were incensed. They called the plumber, thanked him again, but requested him to send a revised bill itemizing the $225 charge.

A few days elapsed, then another bill arrived from the plumber. It read simply: "House Call, $25. Knowing where to bang on pipe, $200."

Enough said.

When we witness the performances of Michael Jordan, Annika Sörenstam, Yo-Yo Ma and Plácido Domingo, we stare in seeming disbelief at how easily they excel. Super-talented artists, athletes, business moguls—and plumbers—all seem to have been born with extraordinary talents.

Well—not so fast.

Maybe something else is in play here.

In 2006, psychologist K. Anders Ericsson wrote in *The Cambridge Handbook of Expertise and Expert Performance* about his research on talented, expert individuals. Lots of commonly held beliefs were dispelled. In one study, at Berlin's elite Academy of Music, he divided the school's violinists into three groups. The first group were stars, destined to become world-class violinists. The second group were strong orchestra candidates. The third group would go on to teach music in local public schools.

Every student had started playing at about the same age. Their differences began to occur when some of them at age 10 started practicing more hours, then added more hours in high school, until they were practicing 30 hours a week at age 20. Ericsson then asked the students to calculate the total hours they had practiced since beginning violin practice.

The results? The first group practiced for 10,000 hours, the second group 8,000 hours, and the third group 4,000 hours. Sounds like the advice my mother gave me: "Work hard and eventually good things will happen."

Practice makes perfect.

Now, you may still be shaking your head—how about the concertos that Mozart was writing at age 6? Amadeus certainly did not have 10,000 hours of practice by that tender age. The fact is, Mozart did not write his first masterwork until age 21, though he had written concertos that were formalistic hybrids of other composers' work from age 6 to 21.

Researchers have studied many different "talented" prodigies in many different fields of endeavor. Each time, the "talent" showed up after 10,000 hours of practice. So, it should come as no surprise that a blacksmith apprentice in centuries past was required to spend seven years with his master before setting up his own shop.

By the time Bill Gates started Microsoft, he had accumulated 10,000 hours of computer time. As an 8th grader in 1968 in Seattle, he began programming just up the street at the University of Washington. Computer terminals there were open late at night and, between 3 - 6 a.m., Bill would sneak out of his house and spend many hours working on programs. By the time he dropped out of Harvard and launched Microsoft, he had already topped his requisite 10,000 hours.

Malcolm Gladwell, in his book *Outliers* (2008), warns that one can innocently learn the "wrong lesson" from Gates' successful entrepreneurship: "Our world only allowed one 13-year-old unlimited access to a time-sharing terminal in 1968. If a million teenagers had been given the same opportunity, how many more Microsofts would we have today?"

Another 10,000-hour example: The Beatles. Between 1962-1964 they performed live more than 2,000 times. Some of their live sessions lasted up to eight hours in a single day. By the time these English moptop lads invaded America in 1964 and topped the charts, they had paid their 10,000-hour dues. How many bands today— even ones around for decades—have performed 2,000 live concerts?

In the world of finance, investment, real estate and asset management today, how many practitioners have the time- and performance-logged expertise?

The 2008-2009 economic crisis resulted from the abuse of debt. You may recall the previous time America abused debt as a nation, during the limited-partnership frenzy of the 1980s. Like the more recent economic meltdown, a similar meltdown occurred for U.S. banks and thrifts that loaned money for new buildings and over-leveraged office space. In the 1980s, just as more recently, many young people fresh out of graduate school with newly minted MBAs were attracted to the banking and real estate industries. They earned six-figure salaries and kept busy churning out new commercial real estate deals.

As often happens after a financial calamity, questions

abound: "How could this disaster happen?" "How did we get into this mess?"

Well—the tongue-in-cheek answer is: "The MBAs know how to run the numbers; they just don't know what they mean."

Wisdom and experience trump youth and inexperience any day.

Over the past decade, neurologists and psychologists have made some remarkable discoveries about how our brains function in obtaining talent and wisdom. Already at our company, these new findings are helping mentor our staff and, in turn, are helping our clients mentor their children and grandchildren.

These new insights are especially important in guiding today's youth to build upon what they love doing and prepare them for the passing of the family leadership torch. They also are important for working with young MBAs, lawyers, doctors and other professionals until they become seasoned professionals.

There are two distinct facets to this learning. One is time spent "exercising" our brains. The other is building myelin insulation in our brains.

Changing the Conversation

What did I just say?

Like many people, I thought for many years that the neurons and synapses in our brains somehow functioned better as we learned and experienced life. But now, the new science of myelin's vital role reveals something far, far different.

Briefly, scientists have discovered that a human being's "talent code" involves a neural insulator called myelin. Some neurologists now consider it the "holy grail" for acquiring skill.

As Daniel Coyle (no relation to Ed Coyle) writes in his book *The Talent Code* (2009), every human skill—"whether it's playing baseball or playing Bach"—is created by chains of nerve fibers carrying a tiny electrical impulse, essentially a signal traversing a circuit.

Myelin's key role is to wrap these nerve fibers "the same way that rubber insulation wraps a copper wire," writes Coyle. In doing so, each signal becomes stronger and faster by preventing electrical impulses from leaking out.

The more we fire a particular circuit, the more myelin optimizes that circuit, and the stronger, faster and more fluent our movements and thoughts become.

One example that Coyle cites: The Link Trainer for aviators. In the winter of 1934, when skilled pilots in the U.S. Army Air Corps were dying in crashes, FDR demanded a solution. Inventor Edwin Link's trainer permitted pilots to practice more deeply, to stop, struggle, make errors, and learn from them. During a few hours in a Link Trainer, a pilot "took off" and "landed" a dozen times on instruments. He could dive, stall and recover, spending hours inhabiting the "sweet spot" at the edge of his capabilities in ways he never could risk in an actual plane.

The military pilots trained on Links were not braver, smarter or luckier. They simply had the opportunity to practice more deeply.

Let's take a look at a baby acquiring the skill of walking. First, the baby holds onto the coffee table, standing, wobbling, and tentatively moving legs back and forth. The baby lets go of the furniture for a moment, then falls down on a padded behind. This goes on for awhile—until one day the baby lets go of the furniture, takes a step, and then another, and topples over again. Junior gets back up with a big smile and tries again. Doting parents rush to child-proof the whole house, now that their toddler is building mobility skills.

More parental smiles, more baby stumbles—and many, many more confident steps. Junior is quickly laying down myelin in the part of the brain that controls movement. Remarkably, the child is being transformed.

Scientists have documented that our subconscious mind can process 11 million pieces of information per second while our conscious mind can only manage 40 per second. You and I don't "think" about walking. We have built up very thick myelin around those walking nerve fibers that make us expert walkers. But our baby can't become an expert walker until accumulating those 10,000 hours of walking skill—usually around age five or six.

Babies are not born with phenomenal walking talent. What they do have is the time to walk, and the passion to learn how to walk.

If people do not love what they are doing, they will never work hard enough to be great at it. In our brains, myelin insulation does not grow unless action takes place. Merely thinking about something is not action. We must *do* the action.

Once again, harkening back to my mentor, Ed Coyle,

who liked to share his grandmother's expressions: "If wishes and buts were candy and nuts, every day would be Christmas."

Now, myelin may sound like an exotic new neuroscience, but actually it's similar to another biological mechanism we use every day: muscles built through bodybuilding. Athletes, musicians, engineers, plumbers, financial advisors—each one, through individualized deep training, sends precise impulses along wires that give signals to myelinate those wires.

They end up, after all their training, with super-duper wires—lots of bandwidth called *talent*.

When Air Corps pilots deep-practiced inside Edwin Link's trainer, they were firing and optimizing neural circuits—and growing myelin and talent.

Passion and continual practice matter greatly. As Vladimir Horowitz, the virtuoso pianist who kept performing into his eighties, put it, "If I skip practice for one day, I notice. If I skip practice for two days, my wife notices. If I skip for three days, the world notices." Repetition is invaluable and irreplaceable.

Why are passion and persistence key ingredients of

talent? Because the best way to build a good circuit is to fire it, attend to mistakes, then fire it again, over and over and over. Struggle is not an option; it's a biological necessity.

Ericsson's research shows that most world-class experts—including pianists, chess players, novelists and athletes—deep-practice between three and five hours a day, no matter what skill they pursue.

So, the whole talent-and-success equation demands three vital prerequisites: Desire to learn, time in the saddle, and doing what one absolutely loves to do. All three must be present to lay down myelin and build talent.

This is exactly what our parents taught us. Dedication, hard work and a great attitude will go a long way to achieving success.

They just didn't express it in terms of brain electric signals and chains of neurons!

The business-advice industry today is full of gurus and novel concepts—some good, some bad. But the neuroscience of myelin is straightforward. Families—and businesses and organizations—are groups of people who are building and honing skills in exactly the same way as violinists and tennis players. The more we embrace the core principles of "ignition" (passion), deep practice and master coaching (mentoring), the more myelin is built and the more success that can result.

Time is of the essence, though. Age does matter. The vast majority of world-class experts start young. While we can learn throughout life, it's a fact that anyone who has tried to master a new language or musical instrument later in life requires a lot more time and sweat to do so.

Too many young people today want too many things too quickly. They need guidance by older family members and seasoned professionals. They need a sense of belonging to family, to community, to nation and to an inclusive stewardship that far transcends themselves. They also need to be allowed to learn the lessons of failure and accountability and, in the process, discipline and dedication.

George Bartzokis, a prominent UCLA professor of neurology and expert on myelin, once posed the question: "Why do teenagers make bad decisions?" Not waiting for an answer: "Because the neurons are there, but they are not fully insulated. Until the whole circuit is insulated, that circuit, although capable, will not be instantly available to alter impulsive behavior as it's happening.

Teens understand right from wrong, but it takes them time to figure it out."

As the lyrics of Crosby, Stills, Nash & Young's hit song of 1970 say, "Teach your children well...."

All of our futures—financially, politically, socially, ethically—will depend upon how well we coach the next generation to passionately excel.

To grow into greatness.

Money, Money, Money

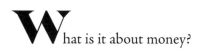

What is it about money?

We must have it to live, but it can also be a terrible burden. When we have enough, life is easy; if not, life is hard. Do we really allow money to exert too much control over us?

Case in point (true story): Many years ago, I met with a young woman who had come into some money. A few years before we met, she had stopped at a gas station to fill up her tank. The time was 6:55 p.m. She filled up, went into the gas station to pay, and impulsively decided to buy one lottery ticket. She paid for it, went back to her car, and tuned into the live radio broadcast of the lottery drawing. To her utter and complete amazement, the announcer read off the six numbers she had selected!

She had just won $6 million. Obviously excited, she

called her fiancé about the great news. After she relayed the news to him and settled down a bit from the shock, her fiancé asked her how she had come to select the six numbers. She replied that two numbers were her birthday, two were his birthday, and the remaining two were the date they first met. His immediate response: "Since two numbers are from my birthday and two from the day we met, half of the numbers are mine and half are yours…so a 50/50 split?"

She was dumbfounded. His first response was how much money he deserved? Needless to say, he quickly became an ex-fiancé. The story only gets worse. Once her friends and family found out about the "good news," her relationships with them changed as well. They expected her to pick up the tab at restaurants and bars. They expected loans or advancements from her for things they wanted. She felt like everyone had an agenda—she was the No. 1 person on their contact lists.

In fact, the change in the relationship she had with her closest friends and family altered so dramatically that she had been seeing a psychiatrist for several years when I met her. She was cagey. She was distant. She was bitter. She was sad. A truly awful story about the trials and tribulations of sudden money.

Money does that to us. We often react strangely to any change in our money state. We feel poor if a large bill arrives in the mail and we need to transfer money from savings or, God forbid, from our home equity line of credit. We get excited when we find a $5 bill in a pocket of a pair of pants we have not worn in awhile. It feels like "found money." This not only happens to the poor and destitute, but to the middle class and to the wealthy as well.

The remarks we make about money offer an intriguing study of the human psyche: "He has every nickel he ever earned." "He has plenty of money—he can afford to lose money in the stock market." "She spends money like it's going out of style." "If I had her money, I could buy a new car, furniture, go on a trip, etc."

Our poems, literature and music are filled with a variety of money messages as well. From Pink Floyd's song "Money":

Money, get away

Get a good job with more pay

And you're O.K.

Money, it's a gas

Changing the Conversation

Grab that cash with both hands

And make a stash....

From the O'Jays' "For The Love of Money":

For the love of money

People will steal from their mother

For the love of money

People will rob their own brother....

From ABBA's "Money, Money, Money":

In my dreams I have a plan.

If I got me a wealthy man,

I wouldn't have to work at all,

I'd fool around and have a ball....

Money can swamp our emotions, resulting in a variety of dysfunctional behaviors. Even though we think we are in control, logical and clear-headed—just throw money into the picture! Should I save more money? Should I spend more money? Can I retire? Should I retire? Live frugally? Spend lavishly? Live for today? Live for tomorrow? The thoughts and questions about money never stop coming at us.

Many mixed messages float out there in the ether. Here are just a few:

A rich man is nothing but a poor man with money.

~ W.C. Fields

It is an unfortunate human failing that a full pocketbook often groans more loudly than an empty stomach.

~ Franklin Delano Roosevelt

Money is a headache, and money is the cure.

~ Everett Mamor

I'd like to live as a poor man with lots of money.

~ Pablo Picasso

I am opposed to millionaires, but it would be dangerous to offer me the position.

~ Mark Twain

Money can't buy happiness, but it can buy you the kind of misery you prefer.

~ Author Unknown

Money is the lifeblood of American commerce. We use money every day—from cash to credit and debit cards, check writing, money wires, and many other ways.

Changing the Conversation

But how well educated are we about money?

In a 2007 survey, only one-third of American credit card-holders who were not paying off their balances monthly knew the interest rate charged on their unpaid balances. A 2008 study revealed that two-thirds of Americans did not understand how compound interest worked. Study after study reveals how woefully uneducated we are about a variety of money issues.

A colleague of mine recently told me about traveling to Las Vegas for the first time with her husband many years ago. They each set aside $40 to gamble with and then call it quits. The first day, she made a little money and felt pretty good. Her husband lost half his money and was a bit down in the dumps. She initially could not understand why he was so mopey until, on the second day, she lost her $40 and felt really bad. The lesson she learned? Never gamble again. The greed and giddiness, and the fear and anxiety, of loss or gain was an emotional roller coaster she no longer was willing to ride.

As a nation, our relationship to money runs in historical cycles. In 1970, around 5% of Harvard graduates went into finance. By 2007, the number increased to 30%—those who expected their first jobs to be in banks.

In 1999, the Glass-Steagall Act—created back in 1933 during the Great Depression to separate commercial banking from investment banking—was dismantled. Earlier in the 1990s, banks, insurance companies and stock brokerage firms had begun offering each other's services. The mortgage industry by the end of the 1990s began to loosen the financial requirements to purchase a home. By the end of 2007, the best and brightest financial minds on Wall Street created about $600 trillion in derivatives in the form of interest rate swaps and credit default swaps.

As our country has experienced time and again in the past—the Great Depression being the poster child—we abuse debt. We seem to *cyclically* abuse debt. We repeat history. We seem to believe that it will be different this time.

We're on a roll in Las Vegas and giddy with excitement.

We Americans are fortunate to have access to capital to buy homes, build businesses, and purchase goods and services on credit. By contrast, take a look at our Third World neighbors to our south. In Peruvian economist Hernando DeSoto's 2000 book, *The Mystery of Capital*, he points out that there are very few small businesses in Mexico and other Latin American countries. The game that is played in Mexico City, as in many other cities in Latin America, involves millions of illegal street entrepreneurs. They open up their stands on the street to sell tacos, only to close them temporarily when the police appear. The police and vendors all know the game. Everyone needs to make a living—just don't flaunt it in front of public officials.

The problem with this game is the maddening inability of the street vendor or any other entrepreneur in Mexico City and elsewhere to establish a legitimate business.

DeSoto points out that, in one Latin American country, it takes up to seven years to obtain a business license—and a total of 168 steps to complete the process through a myriad of government agencies.

The result? A bourgeois society of the status quo. No business license, no access to capital. No access to capital, business dreams die on the streets.

The latest Winter Olympics was held in February 2010 in Vancouver, British Columbia. In the sporting world, Olympic events mark the pinnacle for amateur athletes striving to achieve a usually once-in-a-lifetime goal of obtaining an Olympic gold medal. Some athletes have dedicated the better part of a decade or more of their lives preparing for an event that may last only minutes. —Noble achievement borne out of the human spirit to succeed at something that many of us can only dream about.

Money is absent from Olympic sporting events, other than the host nation celebrating the culture of its people and the beauty of its land. (To be sure, there are professional hockey players on the ice as well!)

In the Vancouver men's moguls competition, one of the favorites to win the event was Australian freestyle skier Dale Begg-Smith—the gold medal winner at the 2006 Winter Olympics in Turin, Italy. Begg-Smith was different from his fellow competitors in several ways. First, he refused to grant non-Australian media interviews— particularly not to Canadian media. Canadian-born but holding dual citizenship in Canada and Australia, he skied for Australia because of past differences with Canadian coaches.

Secondly, he was a millionaire, having made his fortune as a young Internet entrepreneur.

While the personal worth of Olympians is not germane

to competition, for some reason it still can find its way into the reportage. When Begg-Smith declined media interviews, commentators started complaining. In essence, he wasn't "playing the game." At the press conference after winning gold in Turin, Italian reporters pointedly asked his fellow medalists what kinds of cars they drove—compared to Begg-Smith's Lamborghini.

When Begg-Smith objected to this line of questioning about his personal life, press coverage became markedly negative and harsh.

As he continued to be private and standoffish about the granular details of his daily life and interests, matters only got worse.

Money seems to get in the way. It shouldn't—but often does.

Today, examples of dysfunctional relationships involving money abound in our society. From backstabbing competitors on winner-take-all reality TV shows, to corrupt politicians accepting money for votes, to fast-talk sales people selling inappropriate products and services to the public—money can debauch, defile and demoralize.

The solution, of course, is to ensure that money serves

us rather than we becoming slaves to it. Mastering money is a lifelong journey.

Money can damage, maltreat, undermine and disgrace.

Yet—money can also enable, encourage, uphold, facilitate, benefit, guide, innovate, befriend and endow.

We are the freest nation on the earth. We are offered the greatest opportunities. Money helps one to start a business, buy a home, save for retirement, and aid others in need. Look at the outpouring of monetary support for the victims of the Haitian earthquake, Hurricane Katrina, and the Indian Ocean tsunami. Americans— per capita by almost two-to-one over the next closest developed country—are the most generous citizens on the planet.

We believe in helping others, both at home and in foreign lands. We believe deeply in our ideals. We will turn on a dime when someone is in distress. Yet, I wonder when we will match our empathy for human caring with a far better understanding for money's proper role in improving human existence. When will we recalibrate mistaken attitudes and misconceptions about money to see with true clarity what money can—and cannot—do for us?

Money is no substitute for happiness. If we allow it to control our lives, we surely will become a caricature of the travails of the rich-and-famous. Addicted to its beauty, we will end up berating ourselves when its ugly taint and misuse surface.

Money makes the world go round. It's true. We need money to live. It is an absolute necessity for transacting our business and personal lives. What we don't need, though, is money's destructive power invading our lives.

Today, with unprecedented wealth in this nation, the die is cast. Personal and family asset management requires greater awareness and education than ever before. If we are to move forward as a successful people, we must truly understand money, redouble our efforts to place it in its proper service role, and thereby be the masters and stewards of this essential tool of life.

Changing the Conversation—Part 2

My grandfather's wake was held in a small rural funeral home. It seemed the right setting. Grandpa had grown up on a farm outside a remote hamlet. His casket was stationed at the head of the room. The rows of chairs were still fairly empty when we arrived from out of state with our three-year-old daughter. I quietly "visited" Grandpa and then sat down next to my wife and daughter.

The room was cloaked in the quiet whispering of a funeral parlor. At that moment, my daughter turned to her parents and loudly asked, "Why is Grandpa in the treasure chest?" The visitors broke out in small laughter and chuckles. My grandmother smiled even as our daughter continued to look at us quizzically.

In the midst of sadness and sorrow, surprise and laughter—isn't that the evidence of a life well spent?

Changing the Conversation

One man's life runs full circle from birth to death. His great-granddaughter perceives a treasure chest.

Grandpa is the treasure.

His hardy laugh, his practical jokes, his warm embrace, his practical advice and engaging stories had enriched his by then large extended family's lives in countless and incalculable ways.

His quiet wisdom, his fun-loving nature—Grandpa is treasured in family memories by all who had known and conversed with him.

The irony is—when discussing the pursuit of intergenerational well-being—financial treasure pales in comparison to the real treasure.

Oneself.

Our grandfather knew that. While the financial assets he bequeathed were modest, he passed on to future generations his enduring values, morals, principles and sage advice. Today a part of our grandparents is in each one of us, and we pass that on to our grandchildren and then to theirs.

Grandpa had survived the Great Depression and World

War II, fed and sheltered his family during the Industrial Age, received his gold watch, retired at age 65, and slowly faded into the background. His generation never dreamed of living much beyond 70. He left this world the same way everyone does, without his checkbook and billfold. He knew well the saying, "There's no honor in being the richest man in the cemetery."

His was a generation that built stuff. Today we "build" concepts. His was the Industrial Age, ours the Conceptual Age. His was a simpler age, even as tens of thousands of people united to break the German Enigma code, create the atom bomb, and put a man on the moon. Today we have much more complex technology, but with it so many more personal, economic and geopolitical complexities.

There is a need to simplify, to manage, to change—*to change the conversation.*

As our lives have become more complex and our frustrations more pronounced, greater support is needed—*deep support.*

That can only happen if we truly know and understand one another. —If we delve deeply into the complex and at times seemingly overwhelming entrapments of our daily financial, multigenerational lives.

A new kind of conversation must happen and it must be about people—*you and your family.*

In the preceding chapters of conversations, I have sought to offer a transformational structure for framing and addressing the future. Individuals need more than just things. They need trusted counsel backed by deep support.

In today's complex world, value derives from candid conversations and deep dialogue. —From precise words that pierce to the inner core of consciousness with meaning and knowledge. —From wise, innovative solutions matched with carefully mapped, detailed support.

Yes, in my grandfather's time, life was much simpler. The local tailor knew his shirt and suit sizes. The local butcher knew his family's favorite cuts of beef, pork and chicken. The local banker knew three generations of family members by their first names.

That was then. Today, according to some recent polls, a majority of Americans think the country is headed in the wrong direction and is in long-term decline. References are made to political and fiscal system dysfunctions. While there are always reasons for concern during any period, I submit that America's future is exceptionally bright.

Unlocking the frustrated needs of today's individuals and families can unleash the next great wave of business innovation, wealth creation and family well-being.

As authors Zuboff and Maxmin wrote in *The Support Economy*, this will require a profound new *deep support* approach involving mutual trust, long-term relationships, interdependence, intimate knowledge and practical consolidation to ensure utmost value and quality in all decisions.

Such advice, if heeded, poses a bright future. Over the next 40 years, demographers estimate that the U.S. population will surge by an additional 100 million people, to 400 million overall. America's populace will be enterprising and relatively young. In 2050, only 25% will be over age 60, contrasted with 31% in China and 41% in Japan.

In his book, *The Next Hundred Million: America in 2050* (2010), author-geographer Joel Kotkin elaborates on how this growth will change the nation's landscape. Extrapolating from current trends, he sketches out an archipelago of vibrant suburban town centers, villages and urban cores.

The demographic growth will be driven partly by fertility. The U.S. fertility rate is 50% higher than Russia, Germany or Japan, and much higher than China. Kotkin says that Americans born between 1968 and 1979 are more family-oriented than the Baby Boomers before them, and are having larger families.

In addition, America remains a magnet for the world's skilled immigrants, attracting one-half of them. Kotkin notes that between 1990 and 2005, immigrants started 25% of the new U.S. venture-backed public companies.

In his April 6, 2010, New York Times column, "Relax, We'll Be Fine," David Brooks wrote, "The United States already measures at the top or close to the top of nearly every global measure of economic competitiveness. A comprehensive 2008 Rand Corporation study found that the U.S. leads the world in scientific and technological development. The U.S. now accounts for a third of the world's research-and-development spending. Partly as a result, the average American worker is nearly 10 times more productive than the average Chinese worker, a gap that will close but not go away in our lifetimes."

Moreover, as today's generation of Americans leads an economic resurgence, it will do so in a heightened age of social entrepreneurship. Brooks notes that in 1964 there were 15,000 U.S. foundations. By 2001, there were 61,000. In 2007, total private giving passed $300 billion. Participation in organizations such as City Year, Teach For America and College Summit surges every year. "The culture of service is now entrenched and widespread," he writes.

In sum, Americans are strongly independent, culturally diverse and, above all, value freedom. To be American is to believe in the American way of life. Immigrants continue to flock to our shores in pursuit of the American Dream.

America stands on the verge of a demographic, economic and social revival, drawing optimistically upon its many historic strengths.

Learning, earning and *yearning* are life's chapters of preparation, endurance and meaningful exploration in today's America. How we choose to experience each phase—in relation to money—will decide if money's vast power, in turn, ennobles us or enslaves us.

The various conversations in this book have all dealt with the *emotional* (non-financial) aspects of money. Before one can begin to pinpoint the optimal structuring and integration of assets, cash flow, taxes and estates for a family, one must appreciate the *emotional* steps necessary to truly transform financial and family well-being.

Hopefully this book has provided many useful insights into how *today's conversation is changing*—and the critical need to anticipate change, prepare to manage it, and even lead it.

My grandfather understood the power of conversation. Grandpa's life was one of near nonstop conversations about Depression-Era hardship, the ravages of world war, work-a-day toil, national politics and local weather, family endurance and joy.

He taught me that money was mighty important—but as a *means* to an end.

His far greater treasure? His continual conversations with his family.

For him, money booked the travel—but conversation leavened the journey and made it both worthwhile and delightful.

Enjoy the journey.

Seek meaningful conversations.

Bibliography

Listed below are principal texts consulted during the writing of this book.

A Whole New Mind: Why Right-Brainers Will Rule the Future, Daniel H. Pink
(Riverhead Books, New York, 2005)

"A Wondering Mind Heads Straight Toward Insight," Robert Lee Hotz
(Wall Street Journal, June 19, 2009)

Bowling Alone: The Collapse and Revival of American Community, Robert D. Putnam
(Simon & Schuster, New York, 2000)

Brain Rules: 12 Principles for Surviving and Thriving at Work, Home, and School, John Medina
(Pear Press, Seattle, 2008)

The Cambridge Handbook of Expertise and Expert Performance, edited by K. Anders Ericsson, et al.
(Cambridge University Press, Cambridge, U.K., 2006)

Capitate Your Kids: Teaching Your Teens Financial Independence, Dr. John E. Whitcomb
(Penguin Books, New York, 2000)

The Dan Sullivan Question: Ask It and Transform Anyone's Future, Dan Sullivan
(The Strategic Coach, Inc., Toronto and Chicago, 2009)

Changing the Conversation

*Family Wealth—Keeping It in the Family: How Family
   Members and Their Advisers Preserve Human,
   Intellectual, and Financial Assets for Generations,*
   James E. Hughes Jr.
   (Bloomberg Press, Princeton, N.J., 2004)

*The Fred Factor: How Passion in Your Work and Life Can
   Turn the Ordinary into the Extraordinary,* Mark Sanborn
   (Currency Doubleday, New York, 2004)

*Get Out of Your Own Way: The 5 Keys to Surpassing
   Everyone's Expectations,* Robert K. Cooper, Ph.D.
   (Crown Publishing, New York, 2006)

The Go-Giver: A Little Story About a Powerful Business Idea,
   Bob Burg and John David Mann
   (Penguin Group, New York, 2007)

The Golden Ghetto: The Psychology of Affluence, Jessie H. O'Neill
   (Hazelden Publishing & Education Services, Center
   City, Minn., 1996)

Halftime: Moving from Success to Significance, Bob Buford
   (Zondervan Publishing House, Grand Rapids, Mich.,
   1994)

*The Laws of Lifetime Growth: Always Make Your Future Bigger
   Than Your Past,* Dan Sullivan and Catherine Nomura
   (Berrett-Koehler Publishers, Inc., San Francisco, 2006)

Managing in the Next Society, Peter F. Drucker
(Truman Talley Books, St. Martin's Press, New York, 2002)

The Middle-Class Millionaire: The Rise of the New Rich and How They Are Changing America, Russ Alan Prince and Lewis Schiff
(Currency Doubleday, New York, 2008)

The Millionaire Next Door: The Surprising Secrets of America's Wealthy, Thomas J. Stanley, Ph.D. and William D. Danko, Ph.D.
(Pocket Books, New York, 1996)

The Mystery of Capital: Why Capitalism Triumphs in the West and Fails Everywhere Else, Hernando DeSoto
(Basic Books, New York, 2000)

The Next Hundred Million: America in 2050, Joel Kotkin
(The Penguin Press, London, 2010)

Outliers: The Story of Success, Malcolm Gladwell
(Little, Brown and Company, New York, 2008)

Reality Check: The Unreported Good News About America, Dennis Keegan and David West
(Regnery Publishing, Inc., Washington, D.C., 2008)

"Relax, We'll Be Fine," David Brooks
(The New York Times, April 6, 2010)

Changing the Conversation

Selling the Invisible: A Field Guide to Modern Marketing,
    Harry Beckwith
    (Warner Books, Inc., New York, 1997)

The Seven Spiritual Laws of Success: A Practical Guide to the
    Fulfillment of Your Dreams, Deepak Chopra
    (Amber-Allen Publishing/New World Library, San
    Rafael, Calif., 1994)

Special Providence: American Foreign Policy and How It
    Changed the World, Walter Russell Mead
    (Routledge, New York, 2001)

The Starfish And The Spider: The Unstoppable Power of
    Leaderless Organizations, Ori Brafman and Rod A.
    Beckstrom
    (Penguin Group, New York, 2006)

Strengths Finder 2.0, Tom Rath
    (Gallup Press, Washington, D.C., 2007)

The Support Economy: Why Corporations Are Failing
    Individuals and the Next Episode of Capitalism,
    Shoshana Zuboff and James Maxmin
    (Viking Penguin, New York, 2002)

The Talent Code: Greatness Isn't Born. It's Grown. Here's
    How., Daniel Coyle
    (Bantam Dell, New York, 2009)

Think and Grow Rich, Napoleon Hill
    (The Ralston Society, Meriden, Conn., 1937)

The Tipping Point: How Little Things Can Make a Big Difference, Malcolm Gladwell
(Little, Brown and Company, New York, 2000)

Ultimate Kids' Money Book, Neale S. Godfrey
(Simon & Schuster, New York, 1998)

The Virtue of Prosperity: Finding Values in an Age of Techno-Affluence, Dinesh D'Souza
(The Free Press, New York, 2000)

What's So Great About America, Dinesh D'Souza
(Regnery Publishing, Inc., Washington, D.C., 2002)

Wired to Care: How Companies Prosper When They Create Widespread Empathy, Dev Patnaik
(Financial Times Press, Upper Saddle River, N.J., 2009)

The World Is Flat: A Brief History of the Twenty-First Century, Thomas L. Friedman
(Farrar, Straus & Giroux, New York, 2005)

You: Staying Young: The Owner's Manual For Extending Your Warranty, Mehmet C. Oz, M.D., and Michael F. Roizen, M.D.
(Free Press/Simon & Schuster, New York, 2007)

You Were Born Rich, Bob Proctor
(John Wiley & Sons, Hoboken, N.J., 2006)

Acknowledgments

So often one hears the author's cliché, "Writing a book is a labor of love." Well, it's true. Moreover, drafting the text, one feels less the author and more the repository of a lifetime of unexpected, illuminating experiences. My clients have been my classroom. Every single one has taught me something new. This book would not exist without their real-life, day-to-day issues, both financial and non-financial. While protective of their anonymity and privacy, I have drawn deeply upon their great diversity and uniqueness, as individuals and families. All have made me stretch. Every single chapter in this book derives from conversations with my clients. A key lesson they've taught me: In life, it's about the money—and not about the money. That seeming contradiction defines the very essence of the journey to real long-term well-being.

Writing this book required a support cast of many. Without the many thought-provoking, passionate conversations that I've had over 30-plus years of my adult life, this book would not exist. Fortunately, growing up with nine siblings in a busy household where daily conversations with my parents quickly led to decisions and duties, I early learned the value of dialogue. I came to see the power of good communication and steady discipline, and feel the empowerment of family kindness and love. It is hard to imagine how I could have succeeded without my family's support and encouragement.

During the past two decades, Ed Coyle has been a great mentor. He has shared every last bit of knowledge about the financial world and human psychology. In building an outstanding financial advisory practice, Ed set the performance bar high. He is a tough man to work for and with— but what incredible insights and results! A decade ago, he handed me the company's writing torch. He's continually inspired me to write, and has kept me on the rails with expert advice, ongoing encouragement and the occasional exhortation to get back to the manuscript.

Debating, arguing, struggling and succeeding in the business trenches has been a lively journey with my friend and office partner, Kevin Coyle. He plays a pivotal role in assessing my rough drafts and straightening out my disparate thoughts. You will find Kevin in various parts of each chapter, since we live and breathe this business together. Each of us has had similar experiences helping our clients through the financial mine fields. Edward Kelly, my friend and other office partner, is a steadfast source of quiet business strength, for which I am thankful. His teamwork, acumen and dedication to doing everything the right way has greatly supported our business.

I'm grateful to all those who have so kindly and cheerfully provided the daily deep support required of research and writing, especially Kim Frank, Carol Weiss, Vicki Schauer, Jackie Murphy, Ryan Shumaker, Jessica Poisl, Karyn Lachenschmidt, Karen Tuinstra, Rebecca Fragassi, Nora Welter, Marilyn Willard Falkin, Mary Rewakowski, Karen Sanders and Thomas Hines. My mentors and associates, Lynn Lowder, Joseph Janiczek, Joseph Zarlengo, David Goss and Larry Sexauer, have always been there to provide guidance, a helping hand, and (above all) good humor. Special thanks goes to my 9th grade English teacher, Mr. David Stobnick, who gave me a much-needed wake-up call.

Linn Weiss came on board near the end of this project, when I was at my most exasperated, convinced me the book was virtually there, wrestled it from my reluctant hands, worked his editing magic, then helped tackle the usual publishing snarls. A seasoned communicator, he pierced through thickened thoughts and printing complexity—as my editor, helping me tame both.

My deepest gratitude goes to my wife, Debra, who continues to make it possible for me to do work I love and have a real life, all at the same time. At my side for 30 years, she has enlivened and balanced our lives, making sure that work projects don't swallow my life and that I emerge (relatively) sane. Debra is a great listener. Our Saturday morning kaffeeklatsches are the stuff of family legend. When hearing me out, she has helped me crystallize my thinking on many matters.

Alas—so many people to thank. It seems inadequate just to say thank you to all those who have helped me survive this book project, but: Thank you.

While diligent fact checking has been pursued throughout, any manuscript errors herein are entirely my own.

I look forward to continuing the conversation with each and every one of you.

Gary Klaben
July 31, 2010